Preface

In a world that moves at a relentless pace, finding moments of tranquility has become a cherished necessity. It is with great pleasure and a heart full of passion for the natural world that we introduce "Flowers: A Coloring Book for Adults," meticulously crafted by the talented artist and nature enthusiast, Dennis Terry.

Through the pages of this book, Dennis invites you on a journey to explore the serene and intricate beauty of flowers, an adventure that promises relaxation and a delightful reconnection with the simplicity and elegance of nature.

Drawing from years of observation and inspired by the diverse flora that adorns our planet, Dennis Terry has meticulously designed each page with the aim of capturing the essence and diversity of the botanical world. His artwork is not just a testament to his skill as an illustrator but also reflects his deep reverence for nature's unparalleled designs. Each stroke and detail invites you to slow down, to delve into a meditative state where colors flow from your fingertips, filling the outlines with life, and in the process, creating a personal masterpiece that mirrors the vibrant life outside.

"Flowers: A Coloring Book for Adults" is more than just a coloring book. It is an artistic sanctuary where stress and the noise of daily life dissipate, leaving space for peace and creativity to flourish. Whether you are a seasoned colorist or picking up a coloring pencil for the first time since childhood, the floral designs varying in complexity cater to every skill level, ensuring that each person's coloring experience is both challenging and immensely satisfying.

In imagining and creating this book, Dennis Terry has extended an invitation for adults to rediscover the joy and therapeutic benefits of coloring, an activity that transcends age and time. Each page of this book offers a unique floral world to be filled with colors of your choice, encouraging a mindfulness experience that is as unique as the myriad of flowers depicted within its pages.

We invite you to immerse yourself in the pages of "Flowers: A Coloring Book for Adults." Let your creative spirit blossom as you bring to life the exquisite details of each illustration. May this book be a reminder of the beauty that surrounds us and the calm that creativity can bring into our lives. Let each page be a step on a journey towards relaxation, a moment of disconnect from the hustle and bustle, and a personal tribute to the enduring beauty of flowers.

Welcome to your floral escape.

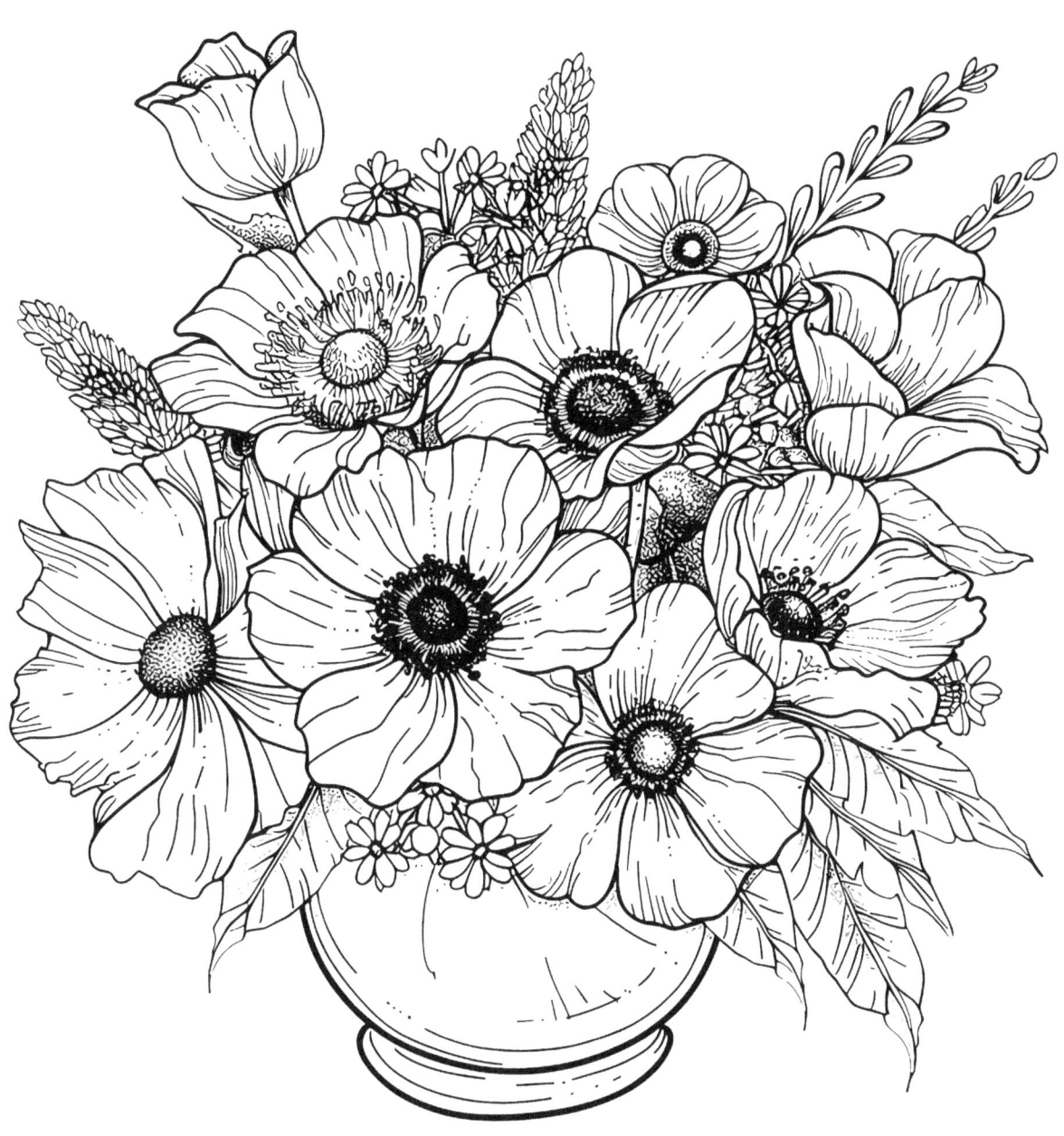

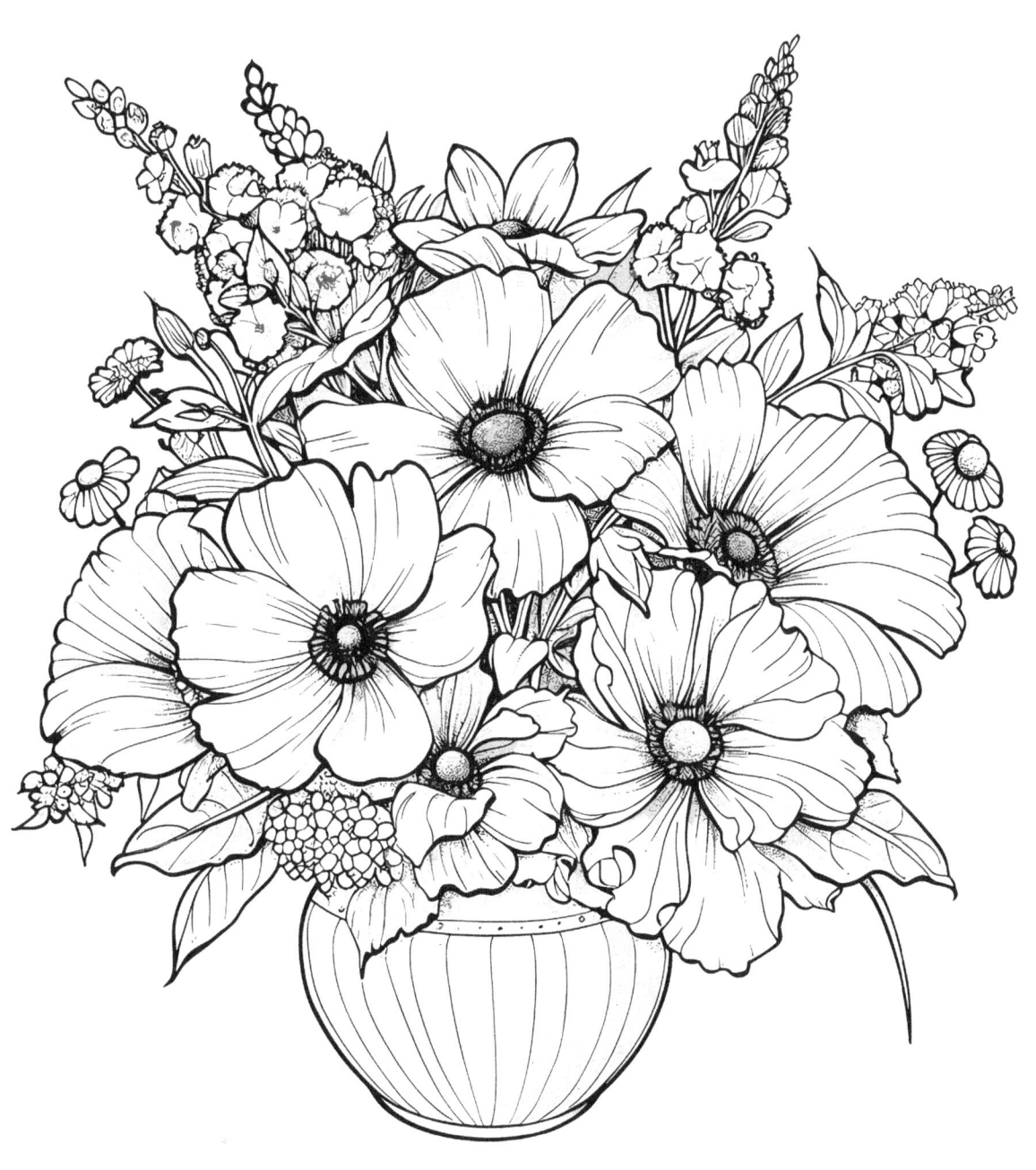

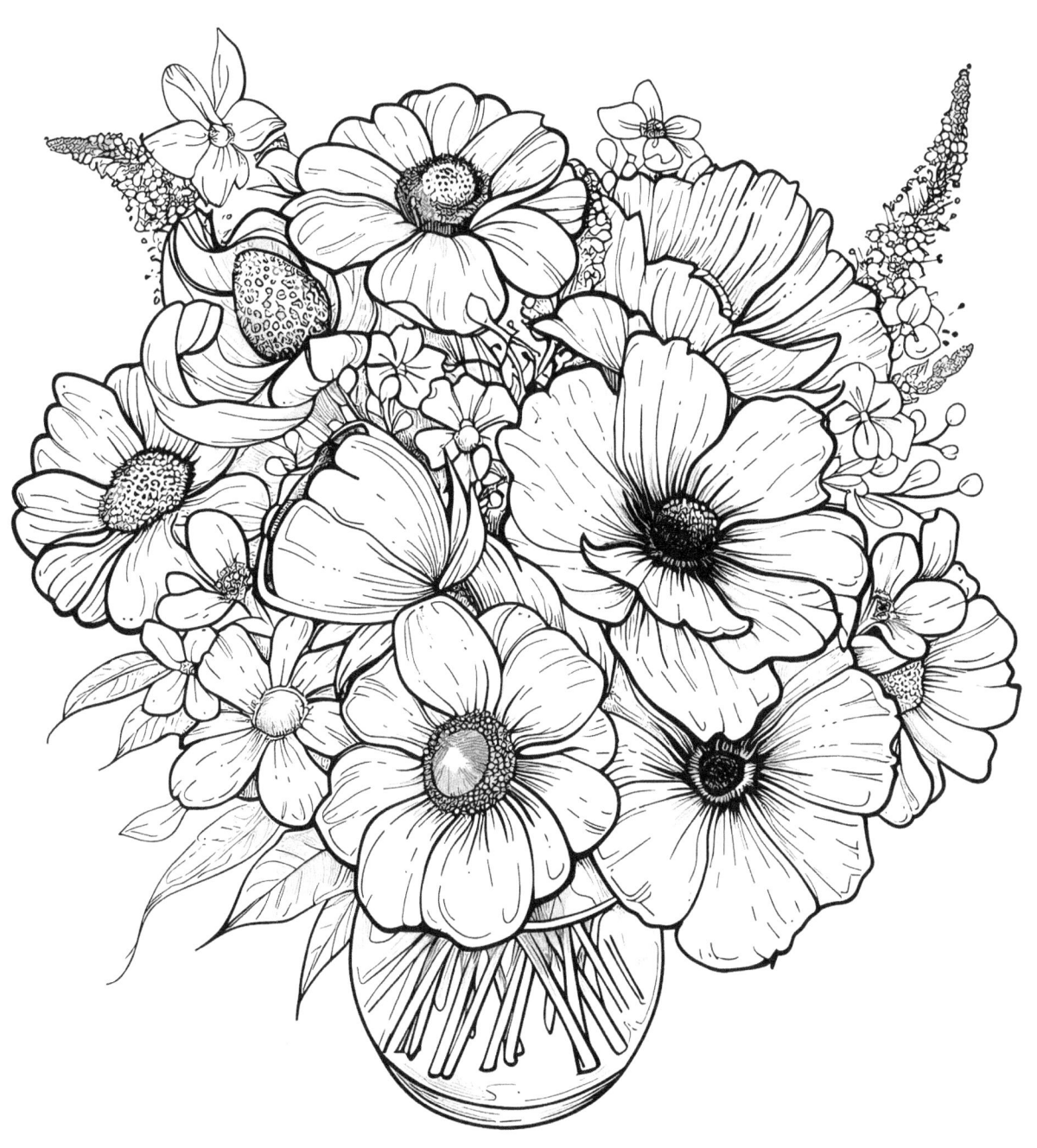

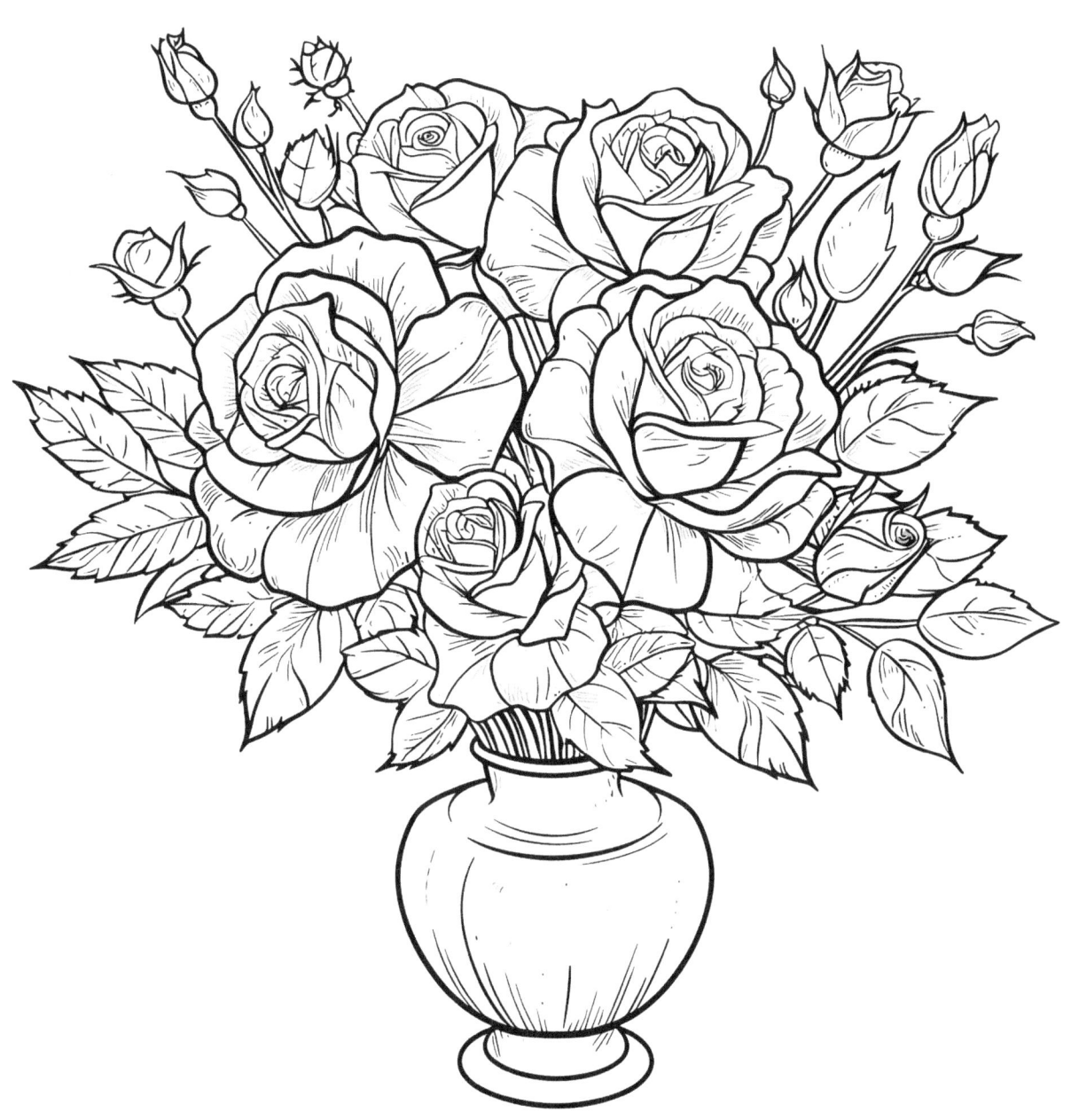

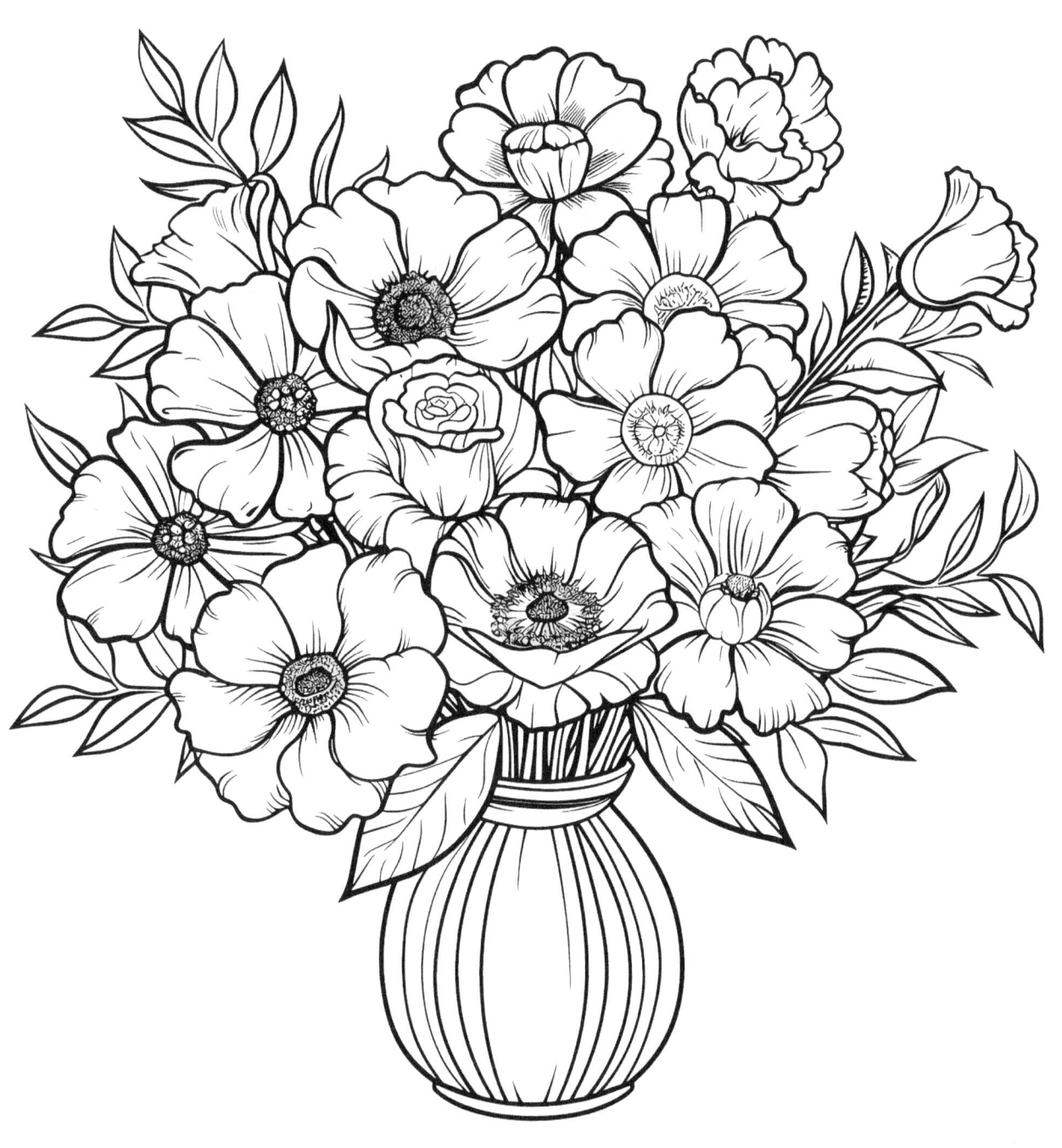

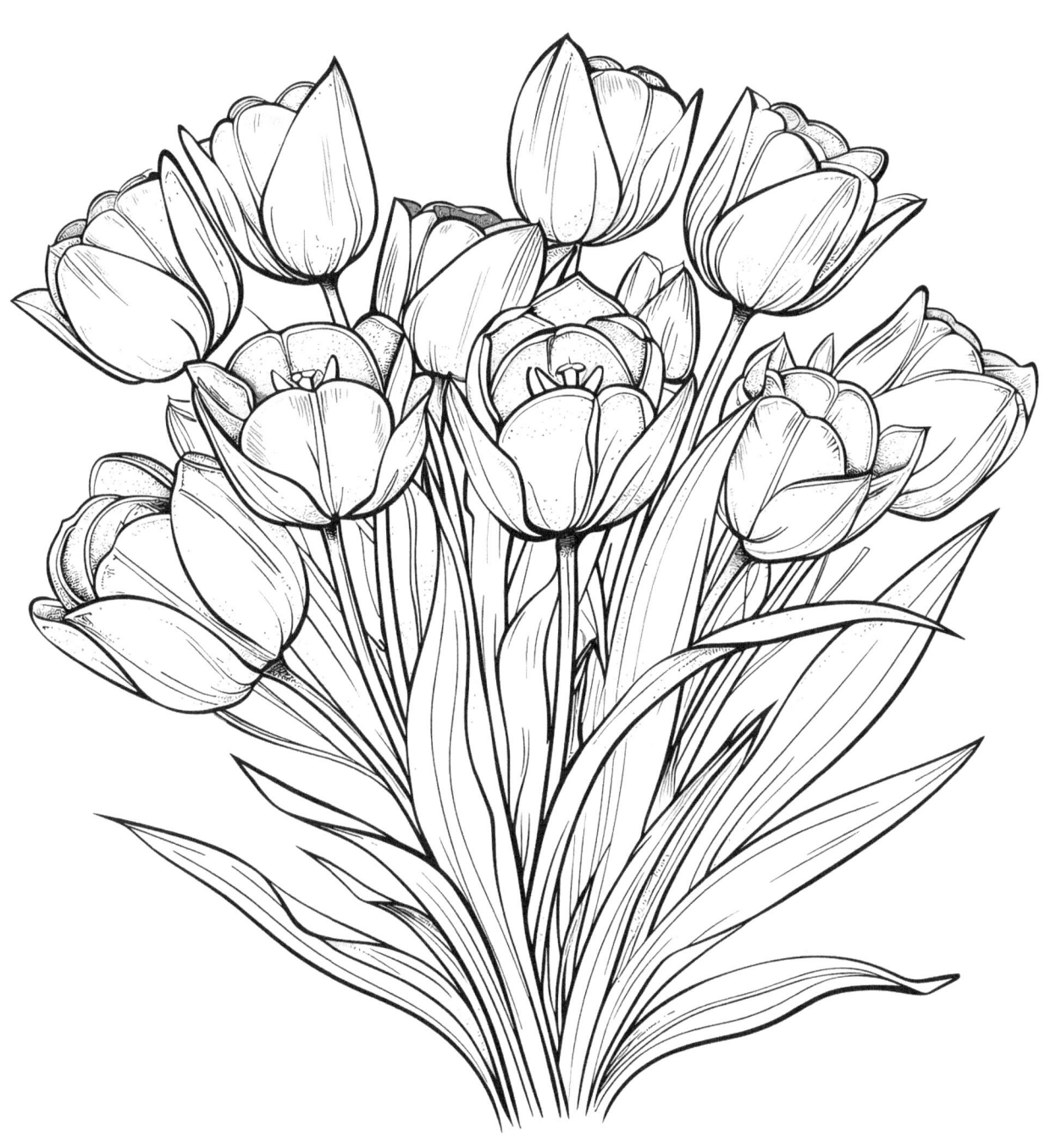

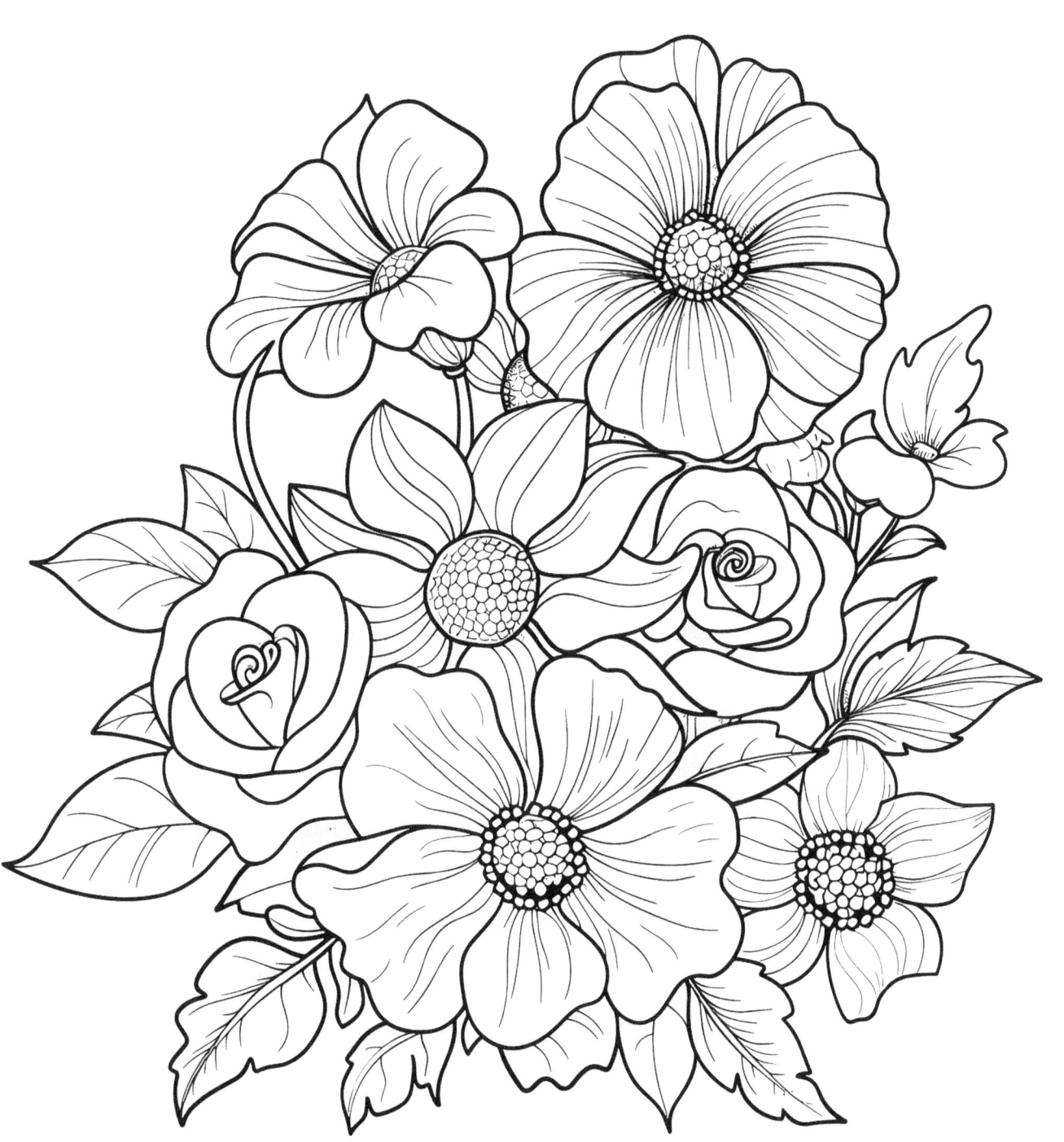

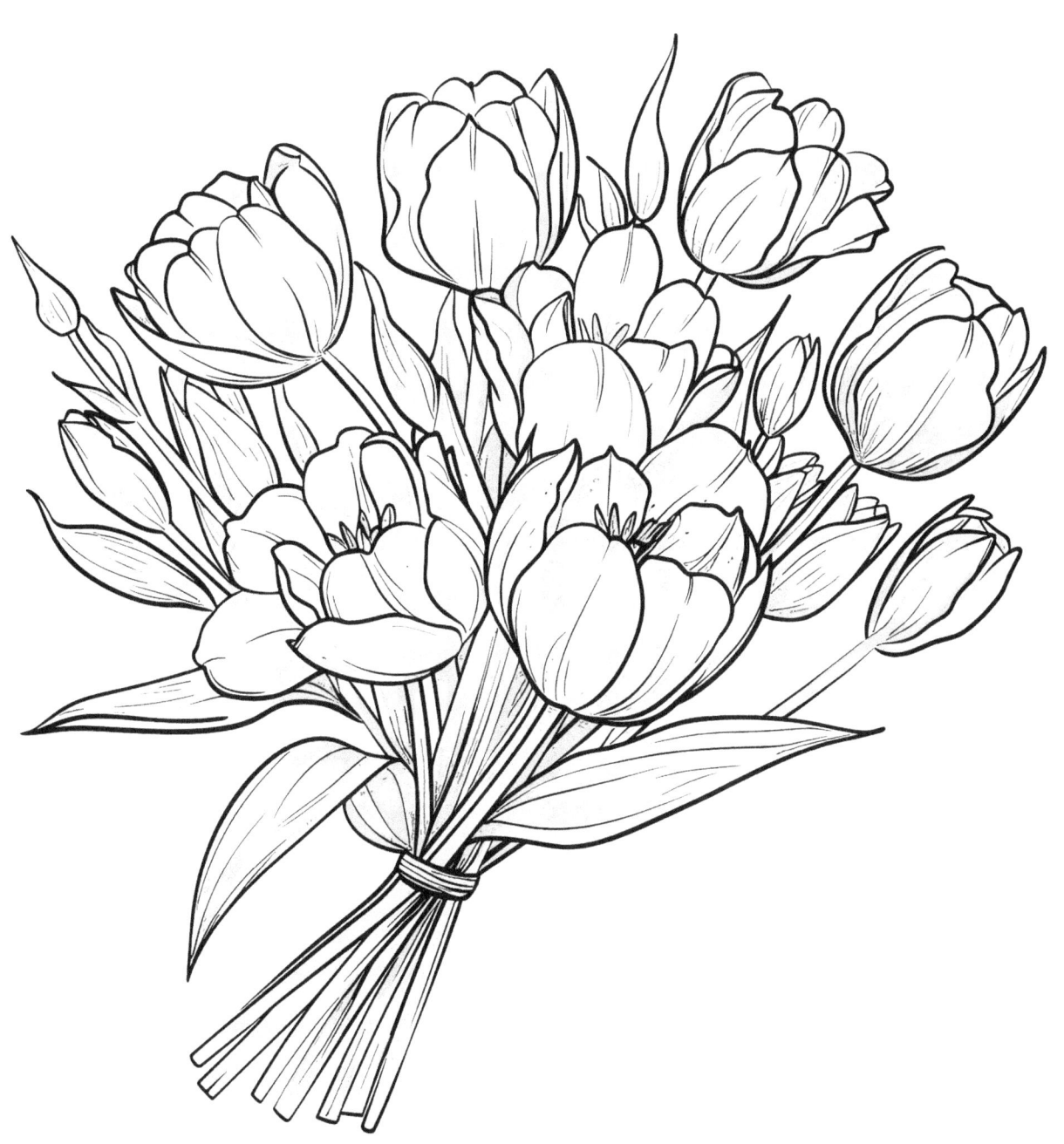

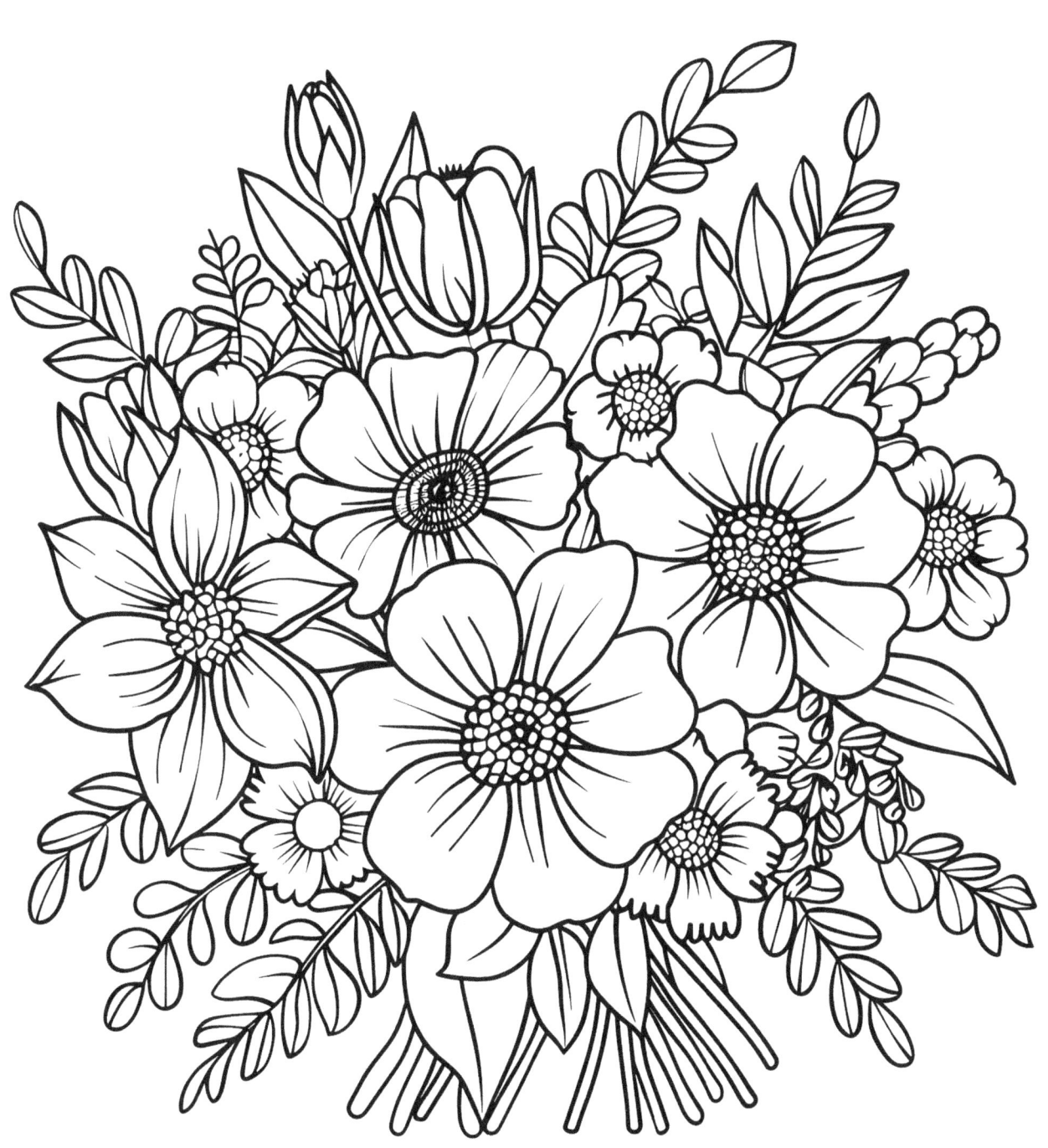

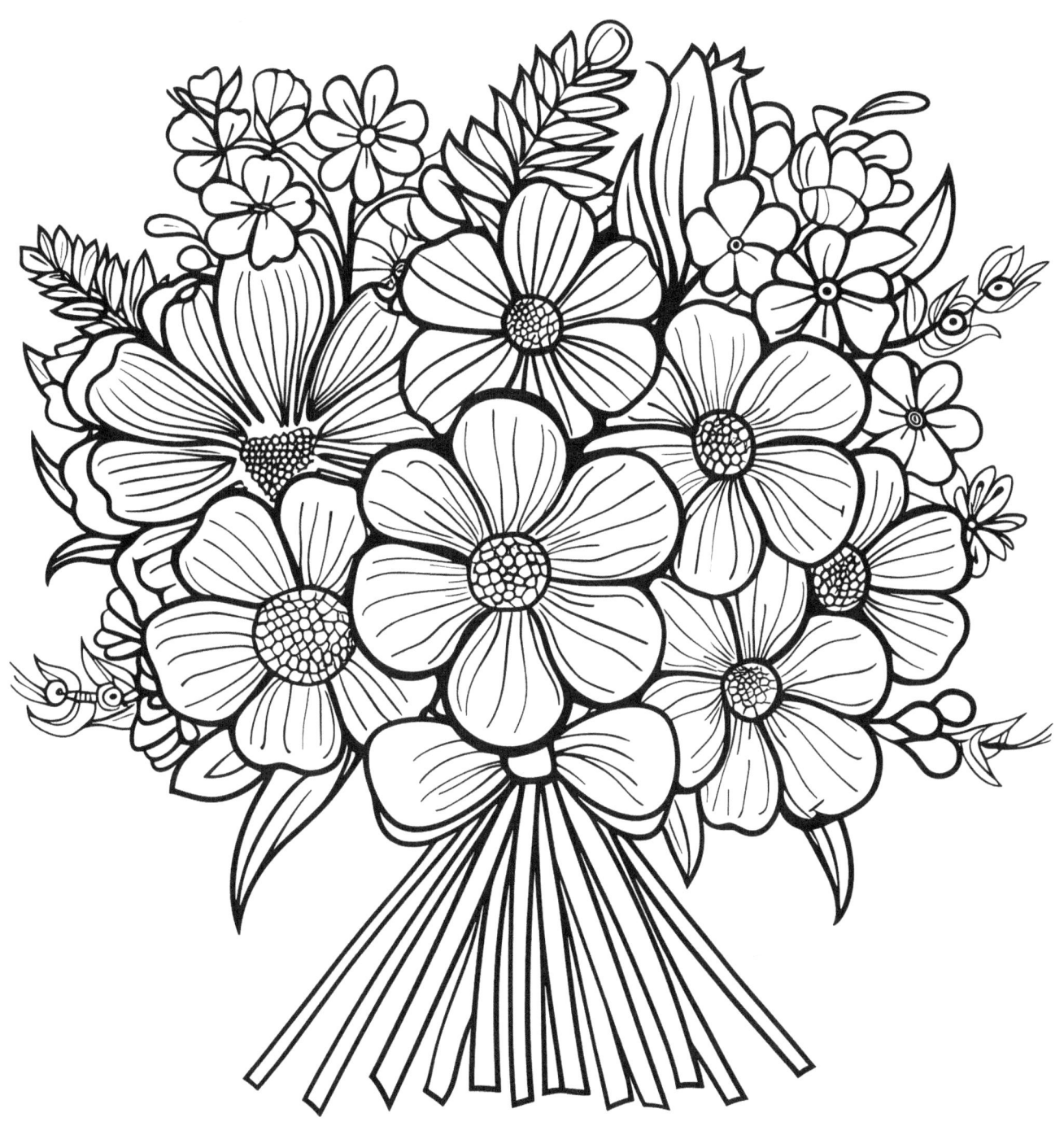

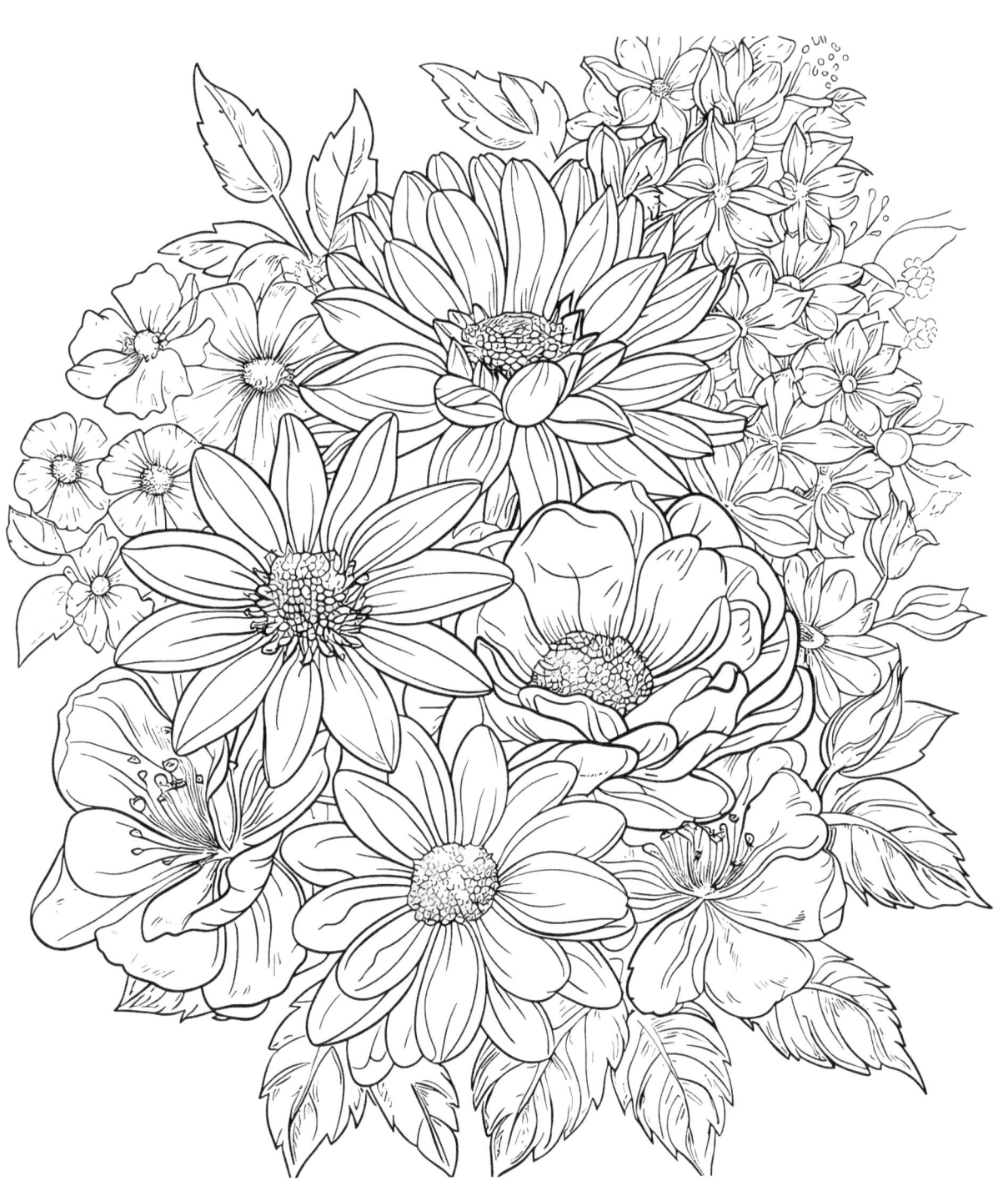

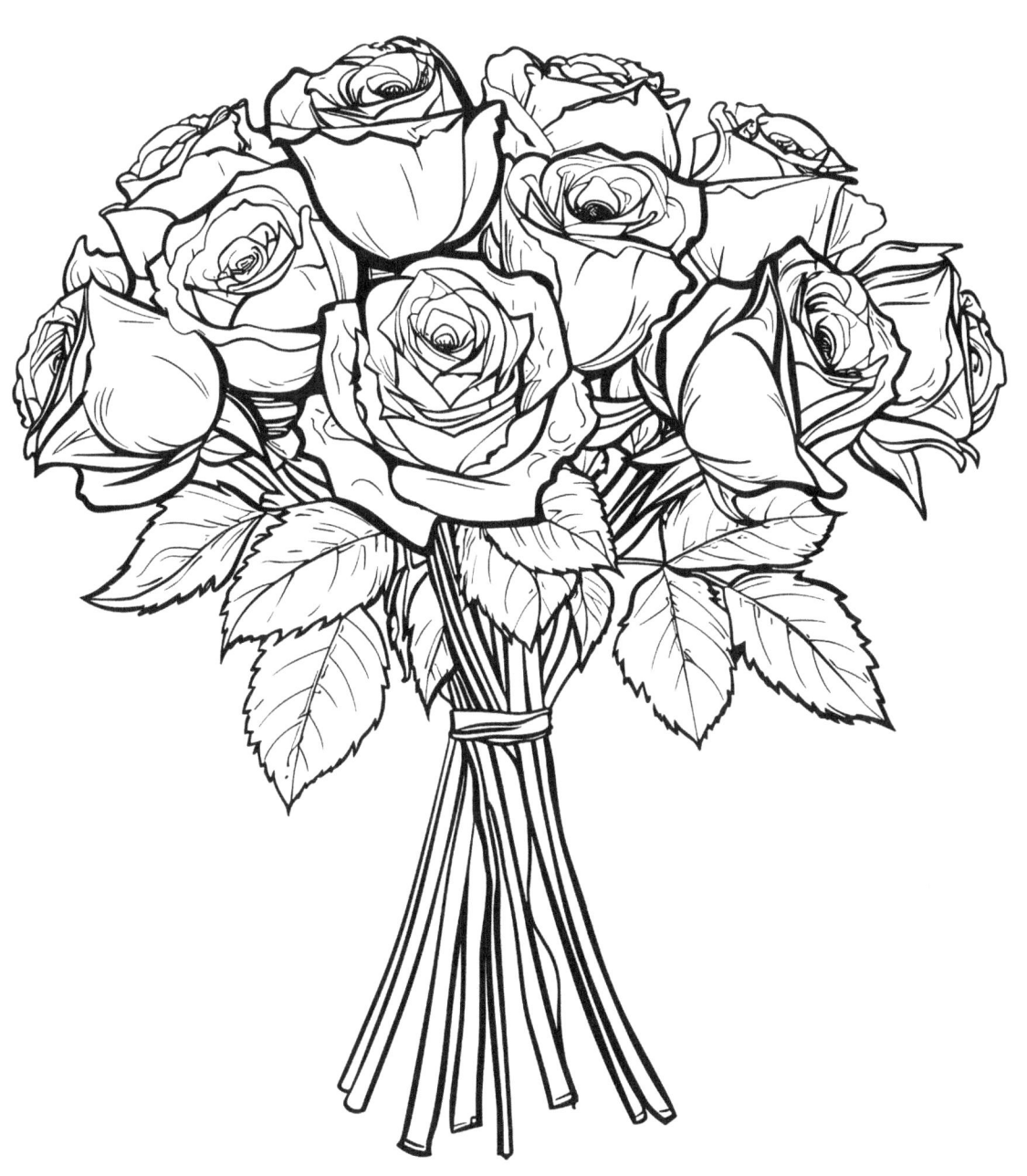

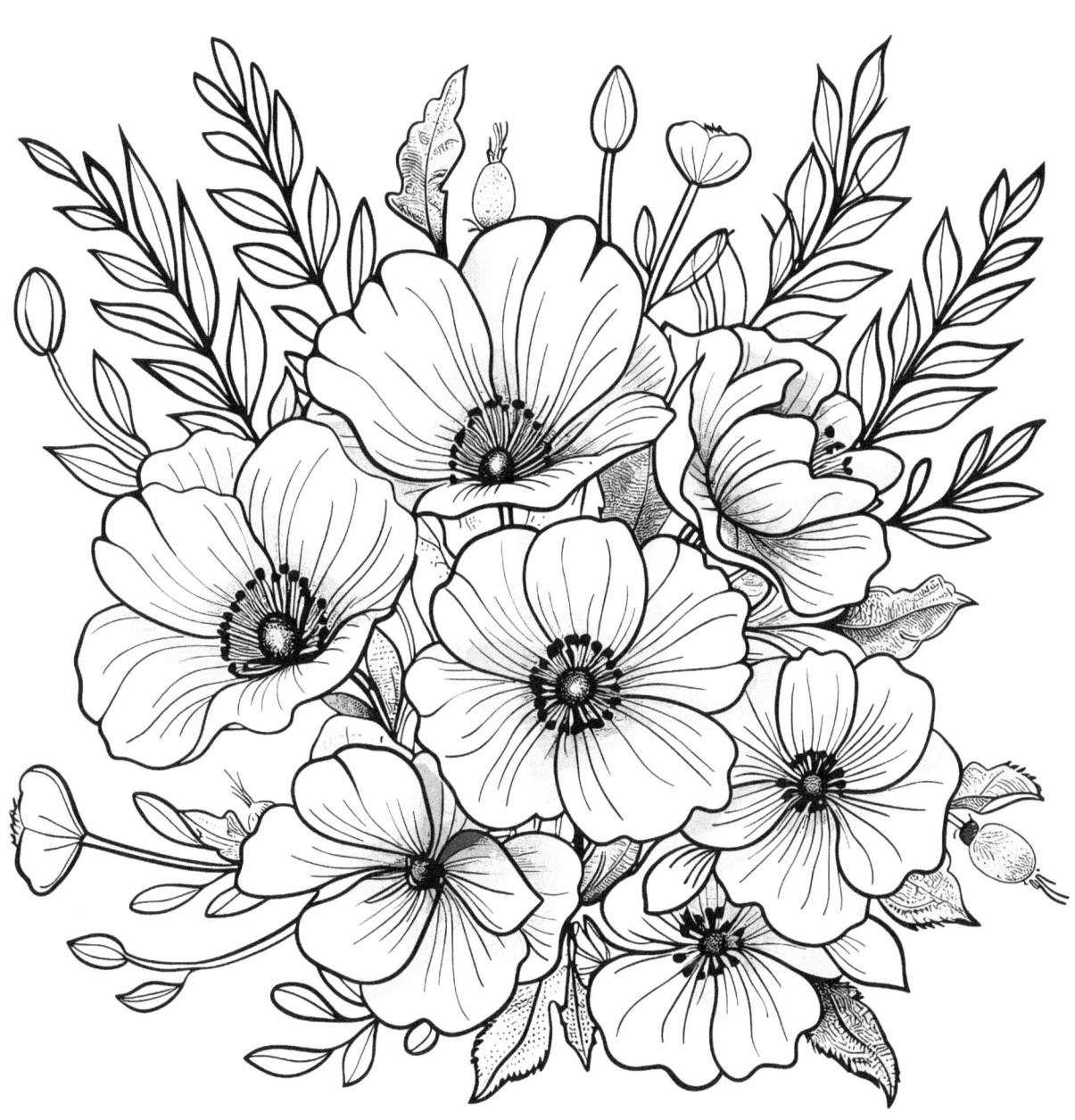

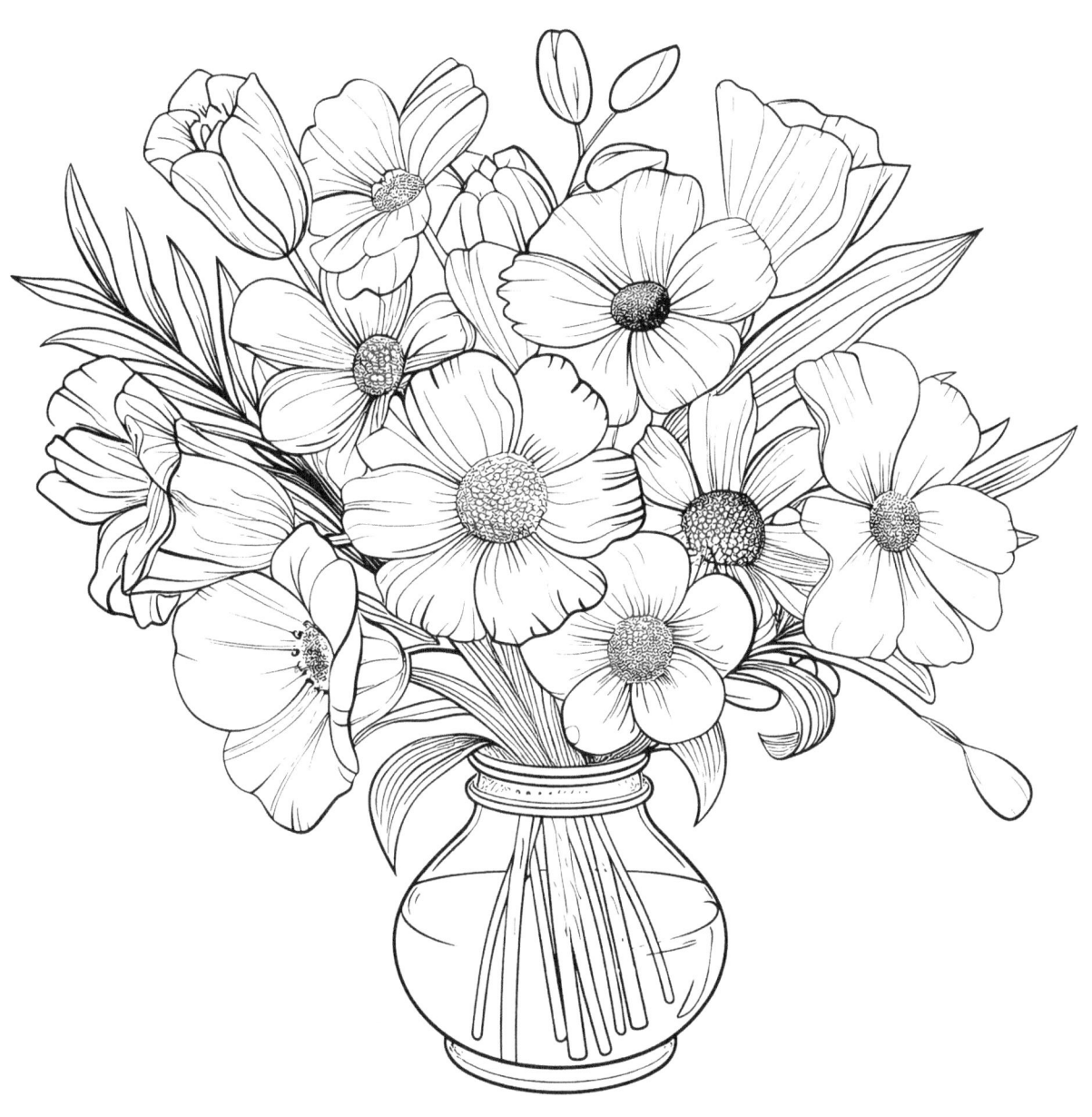

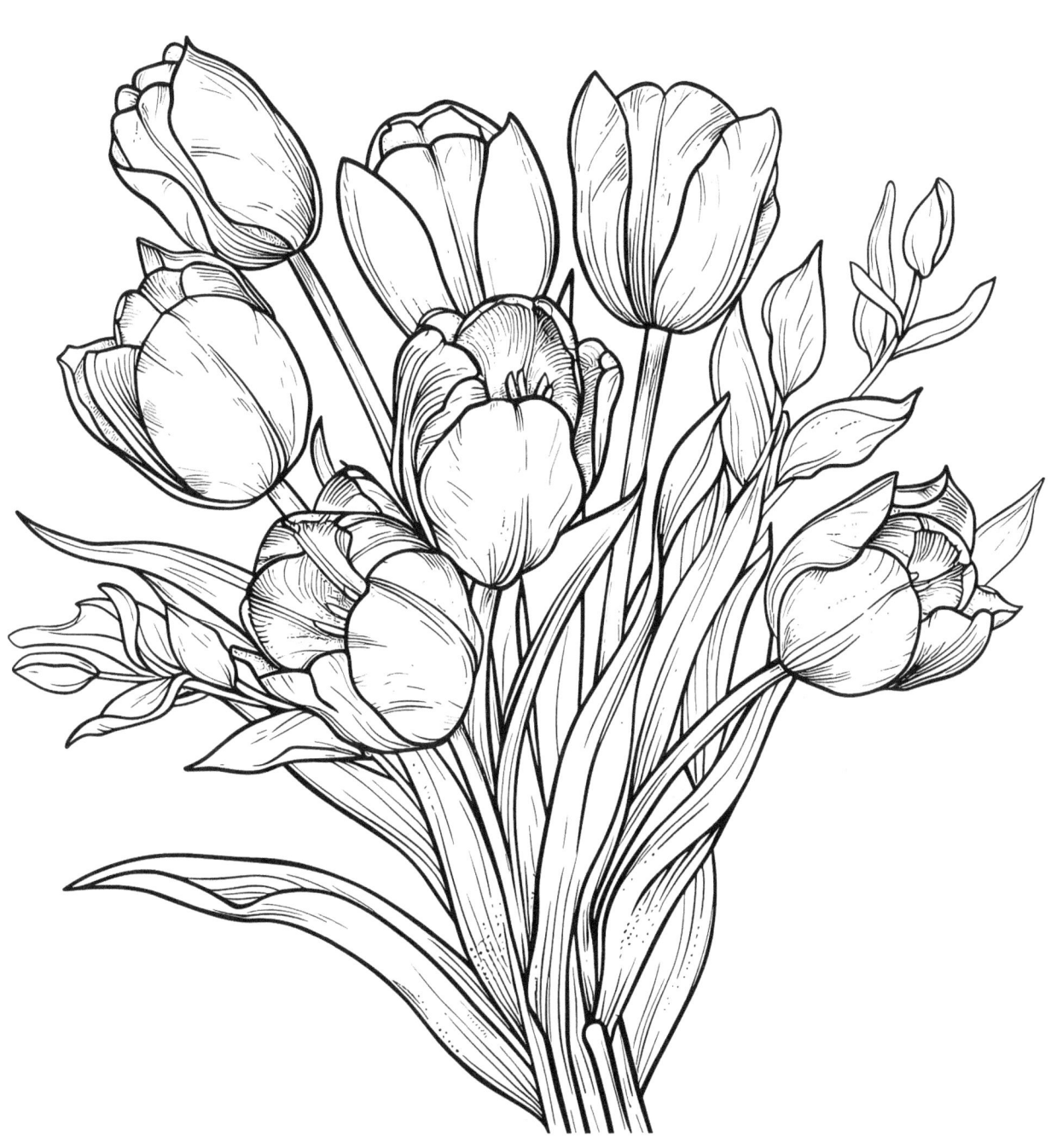

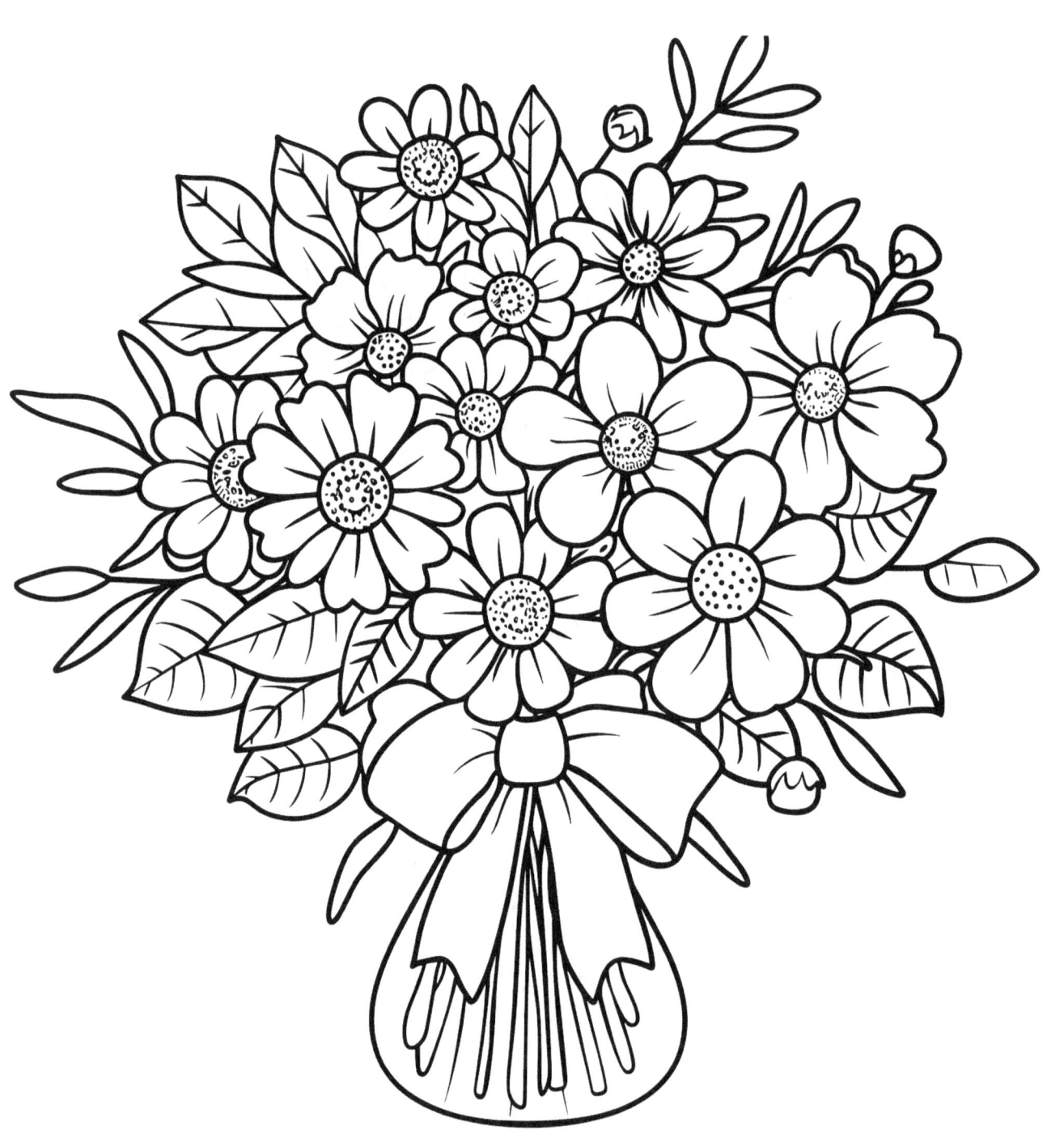

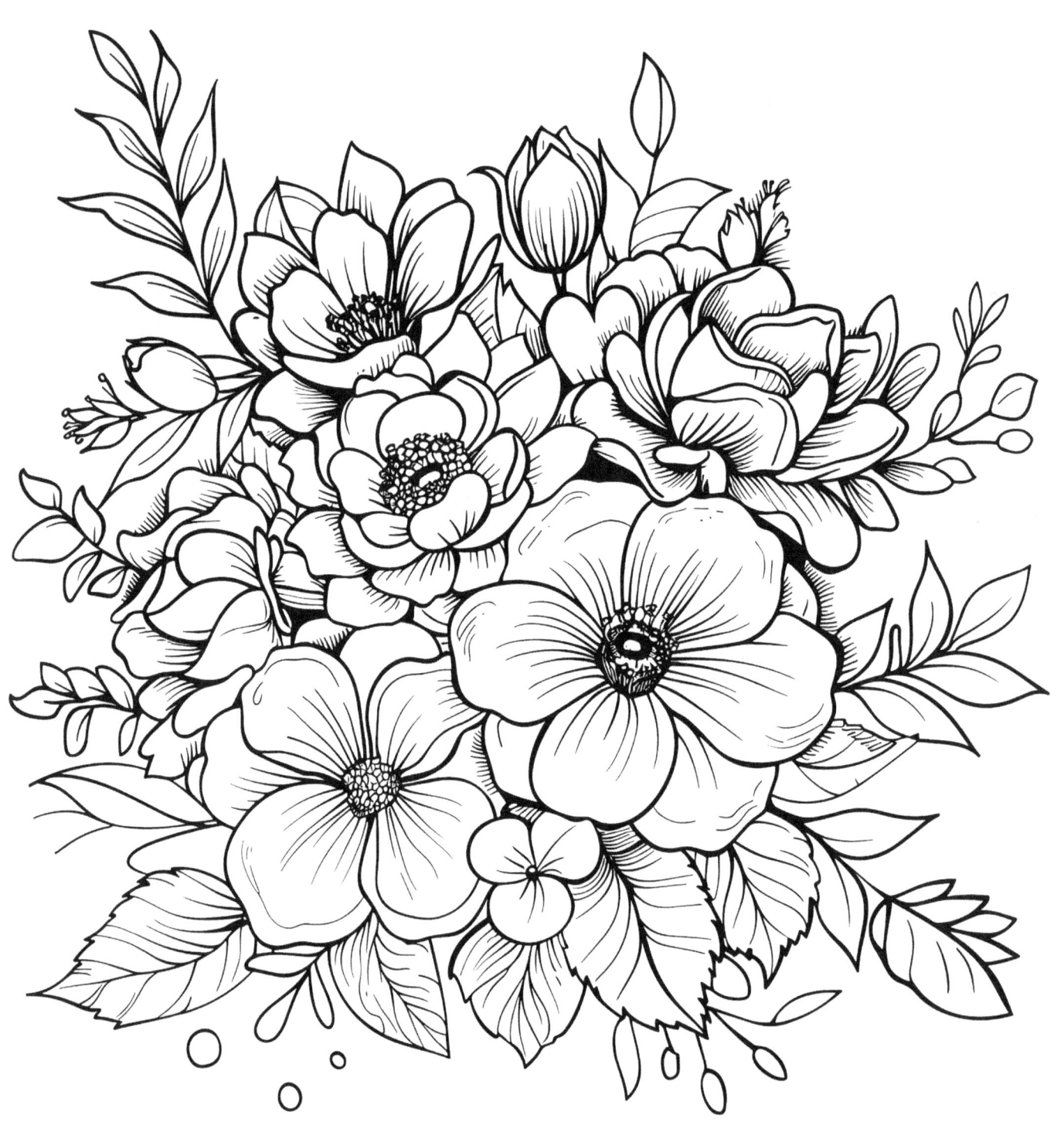

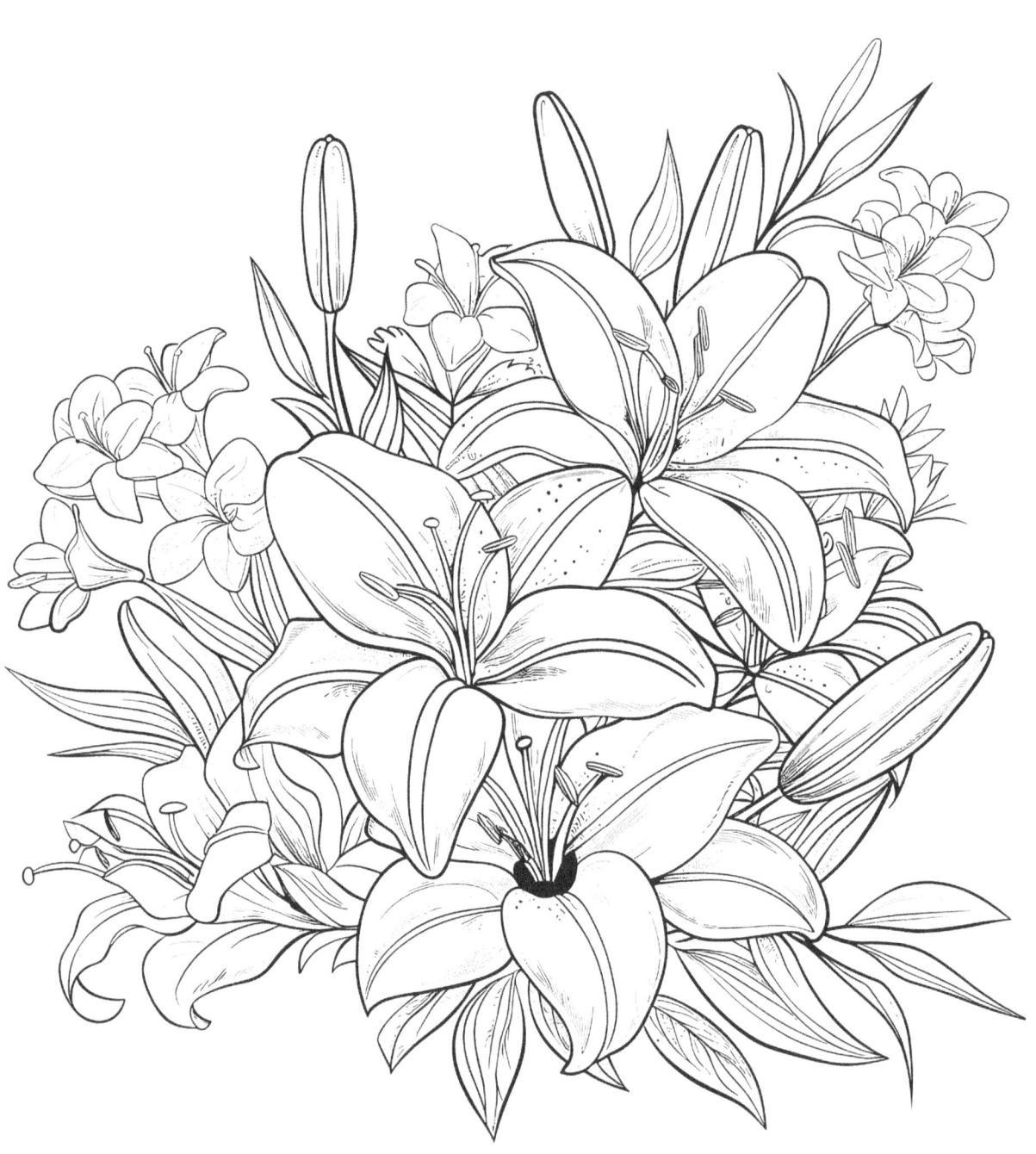

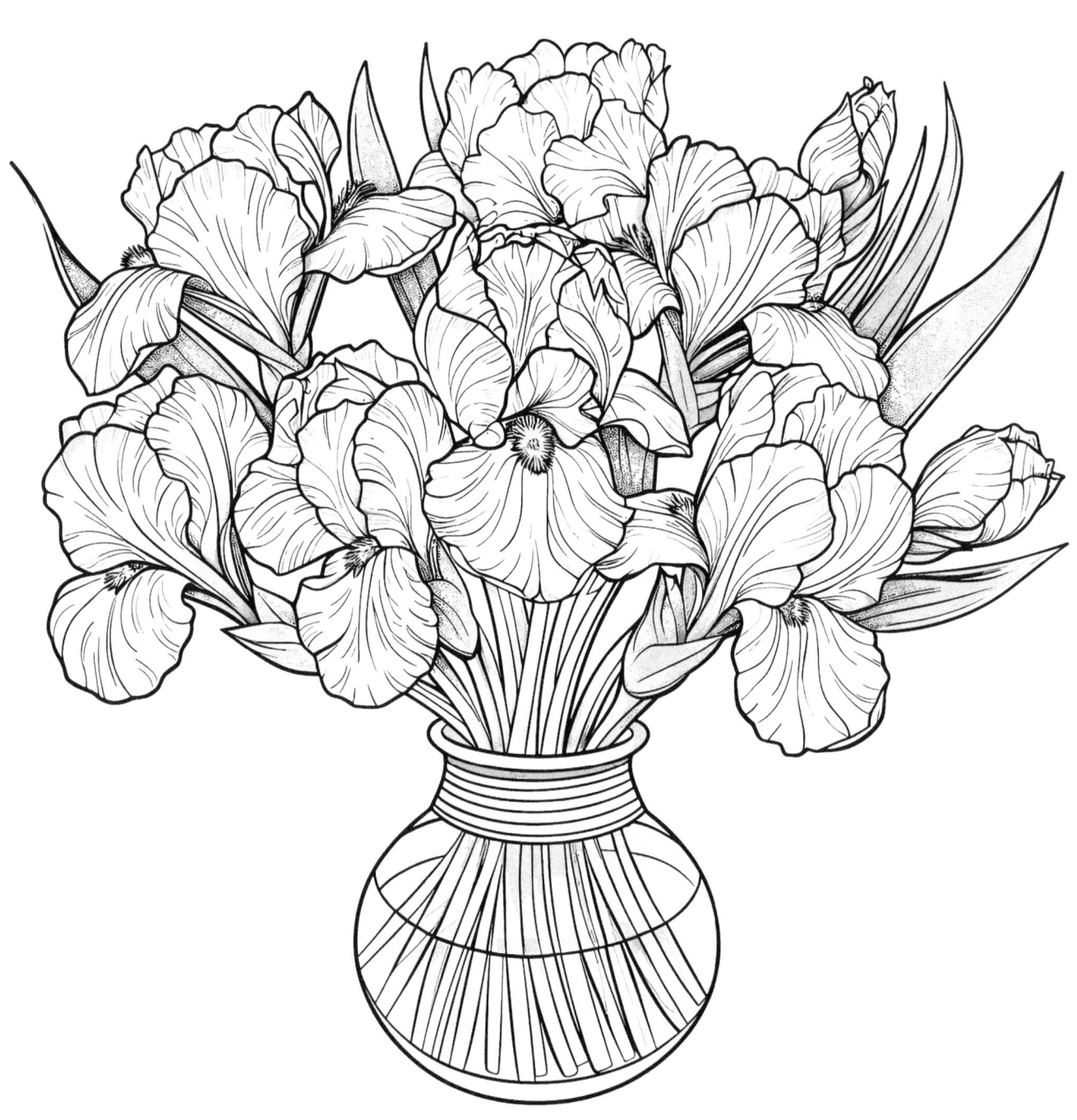

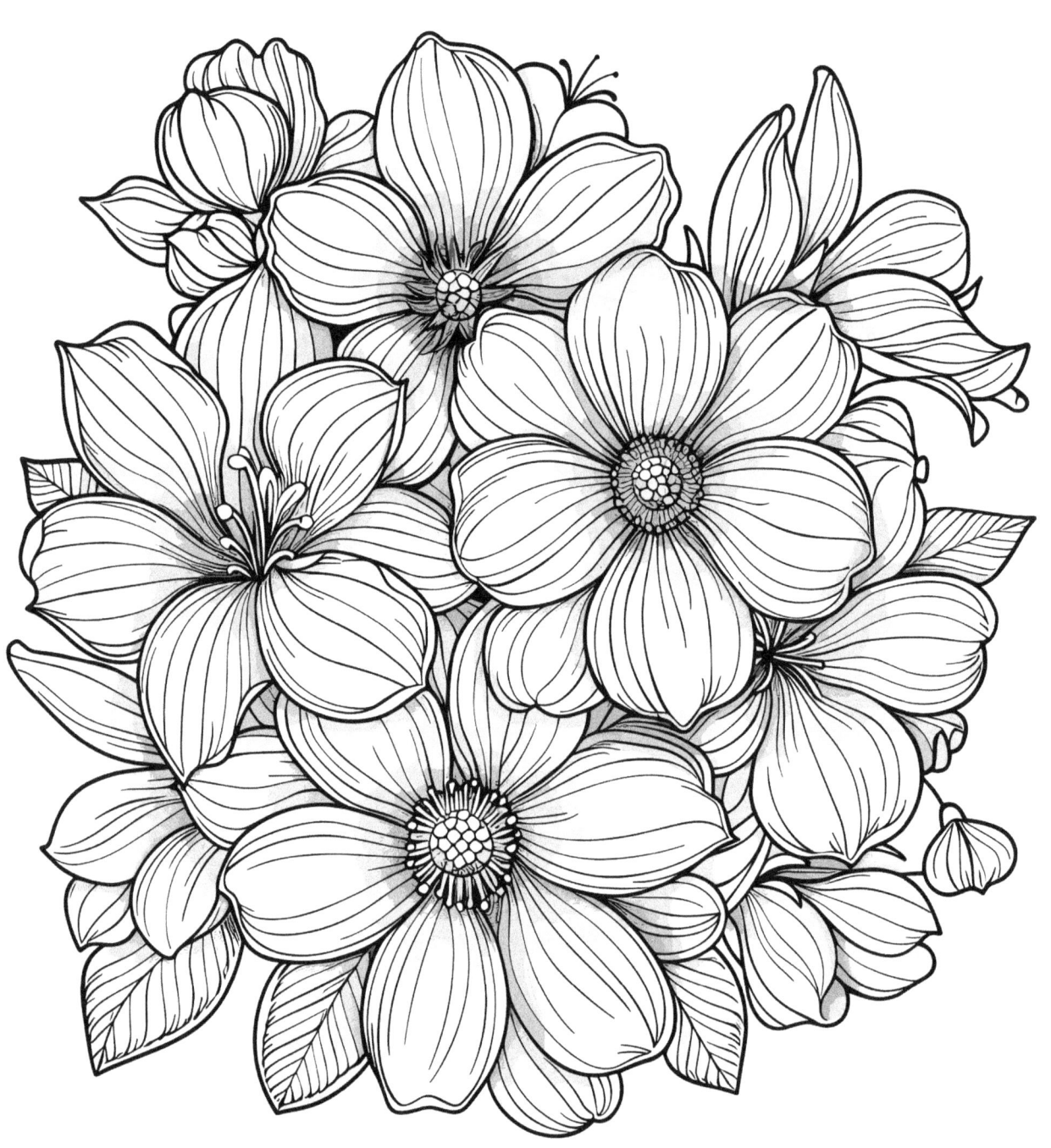

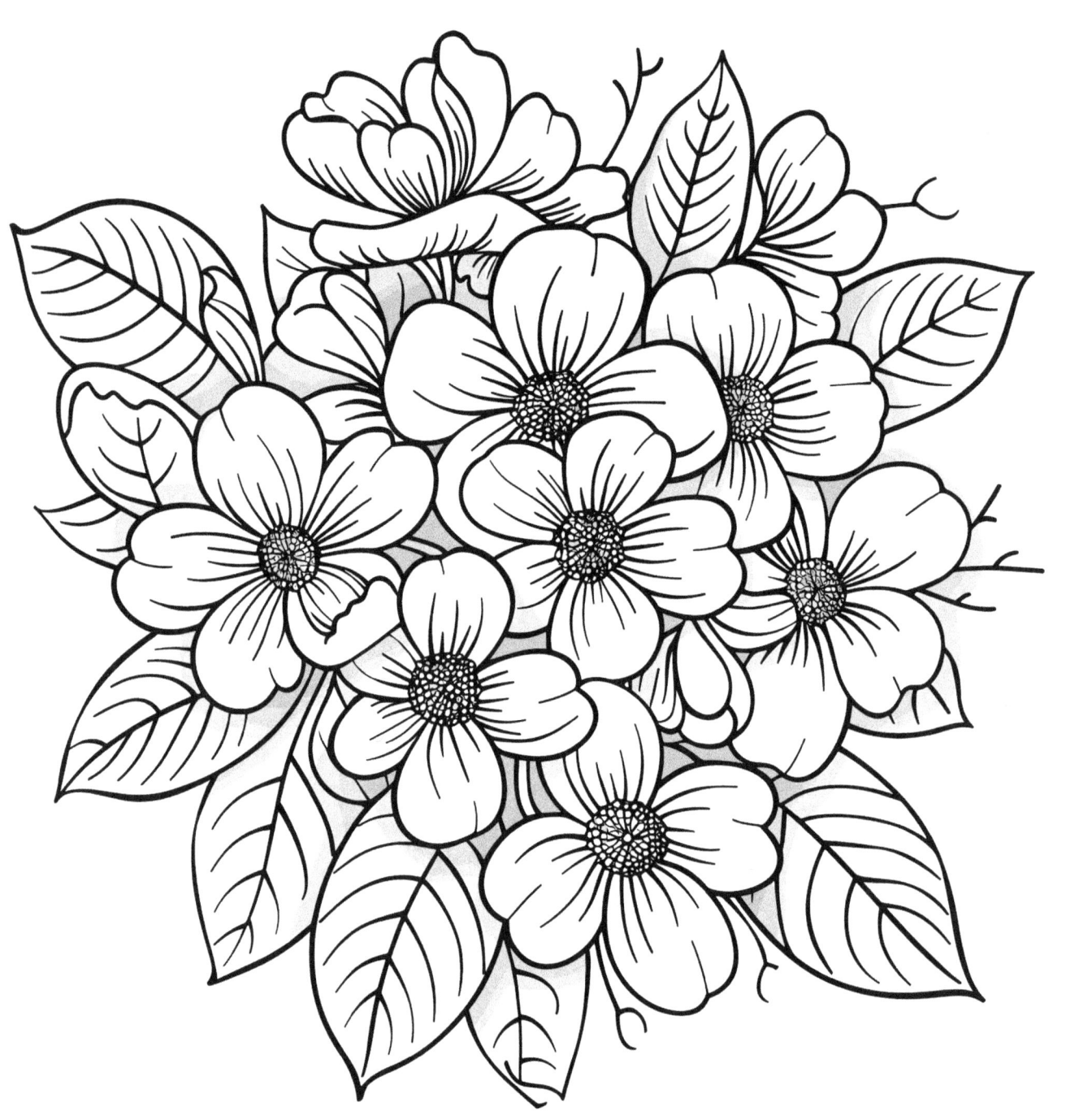

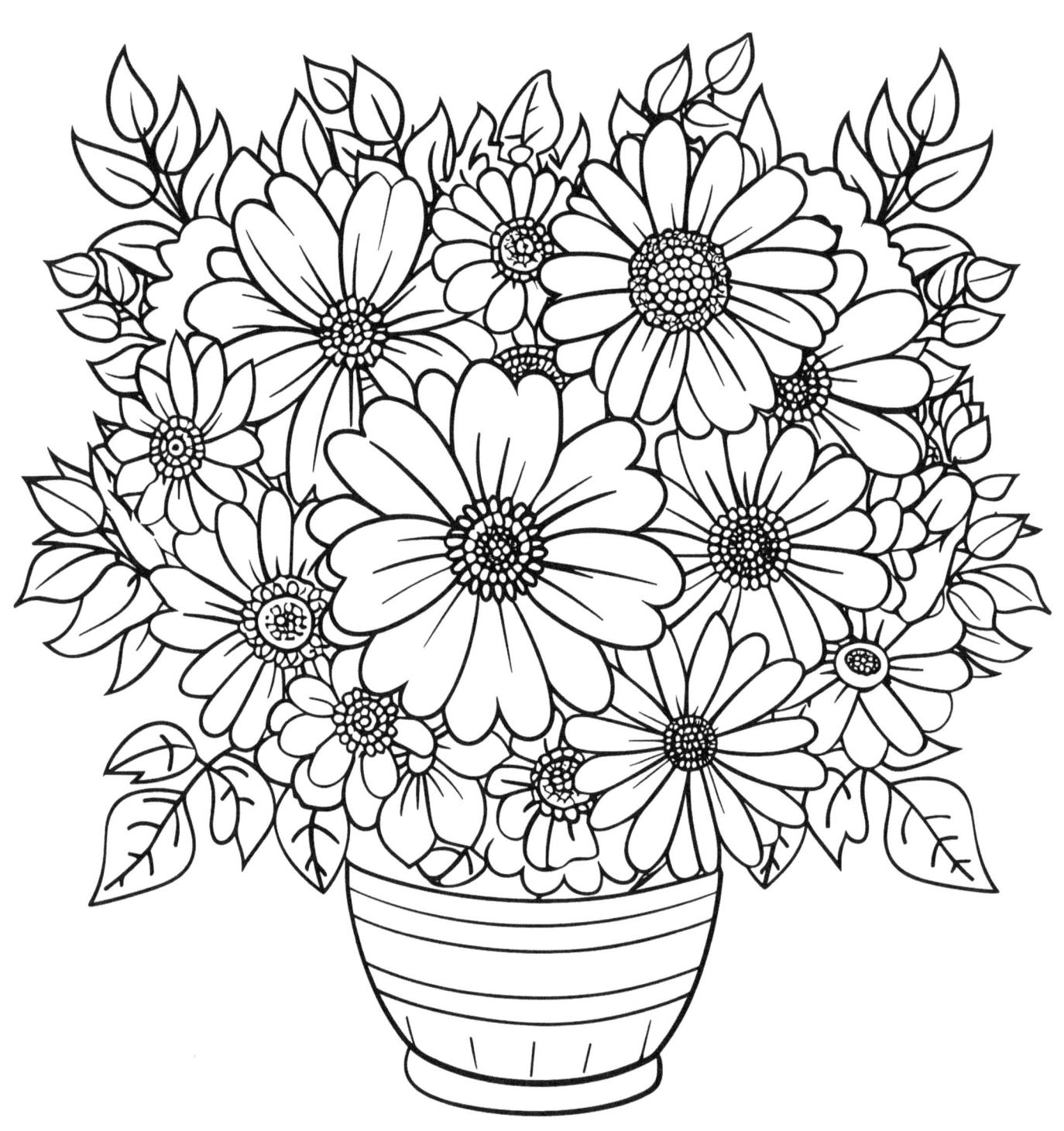

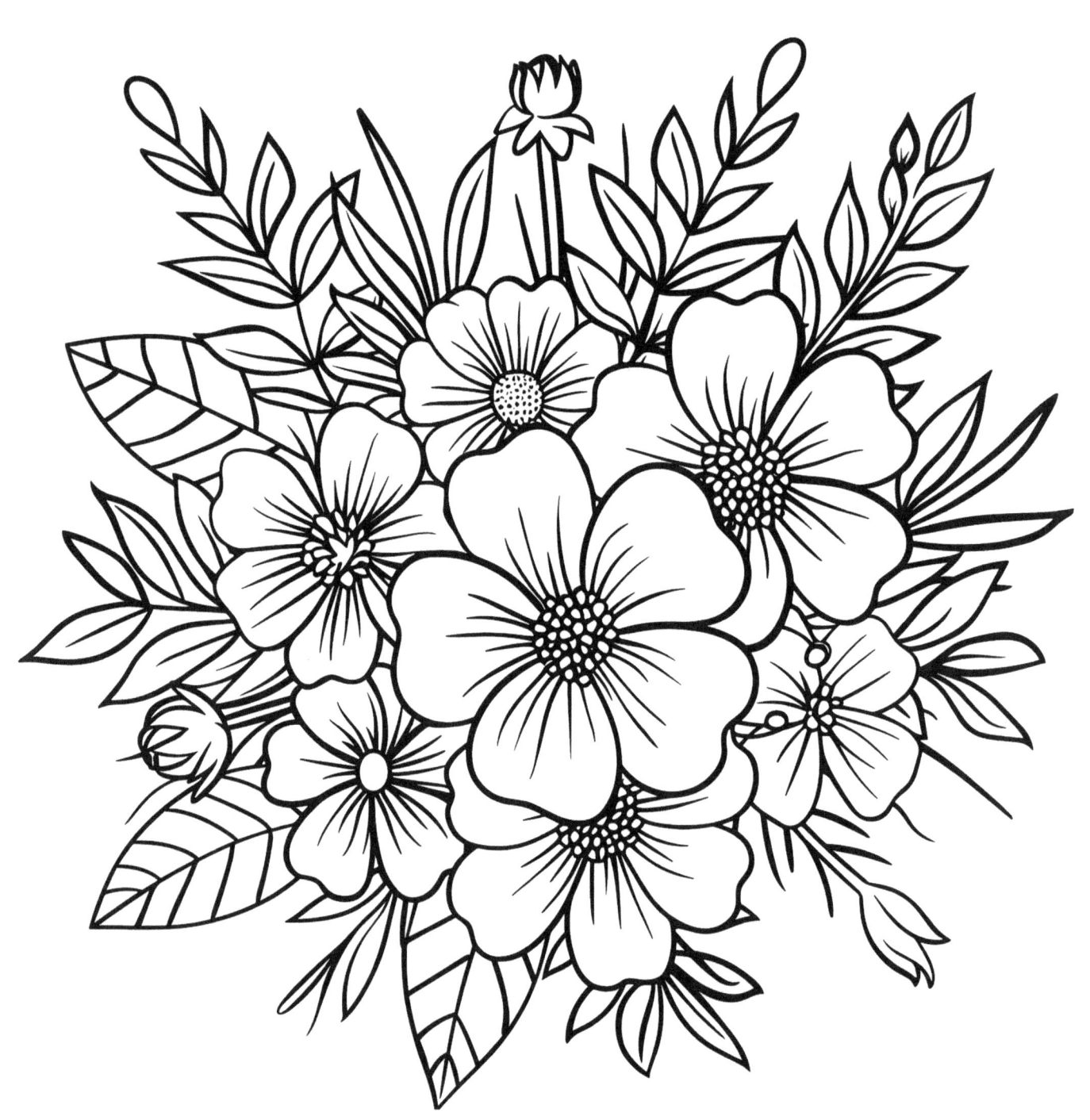

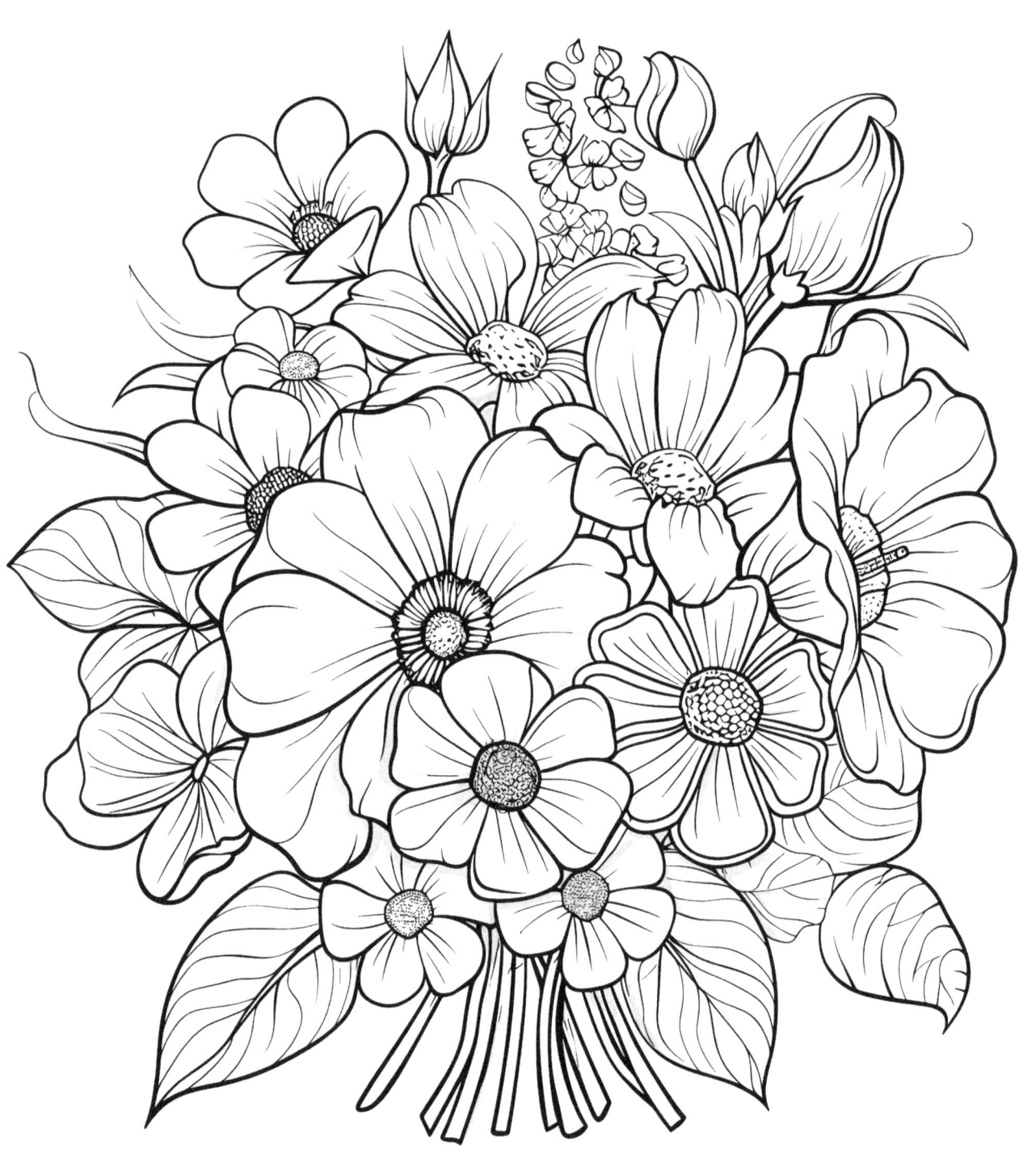

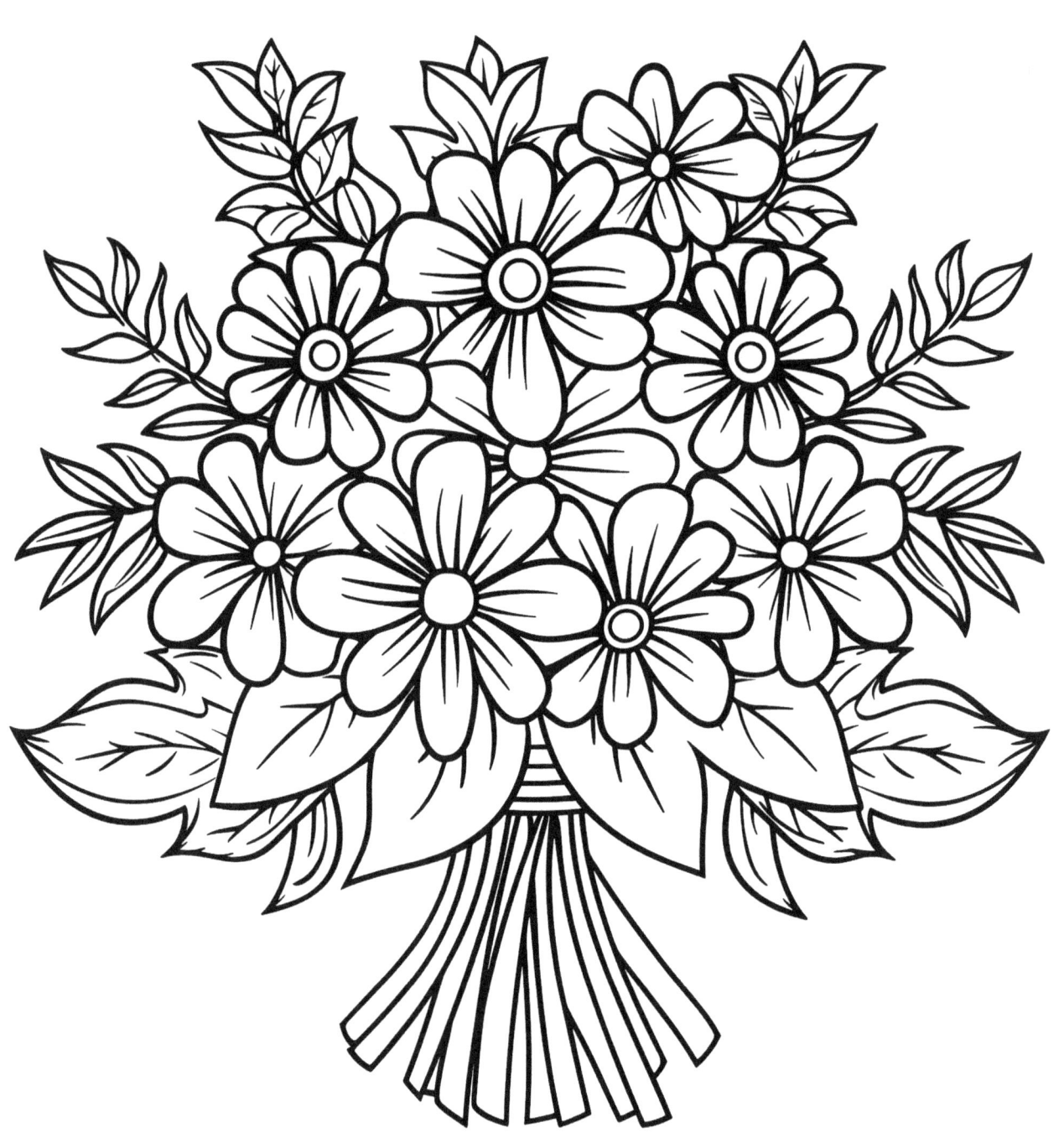

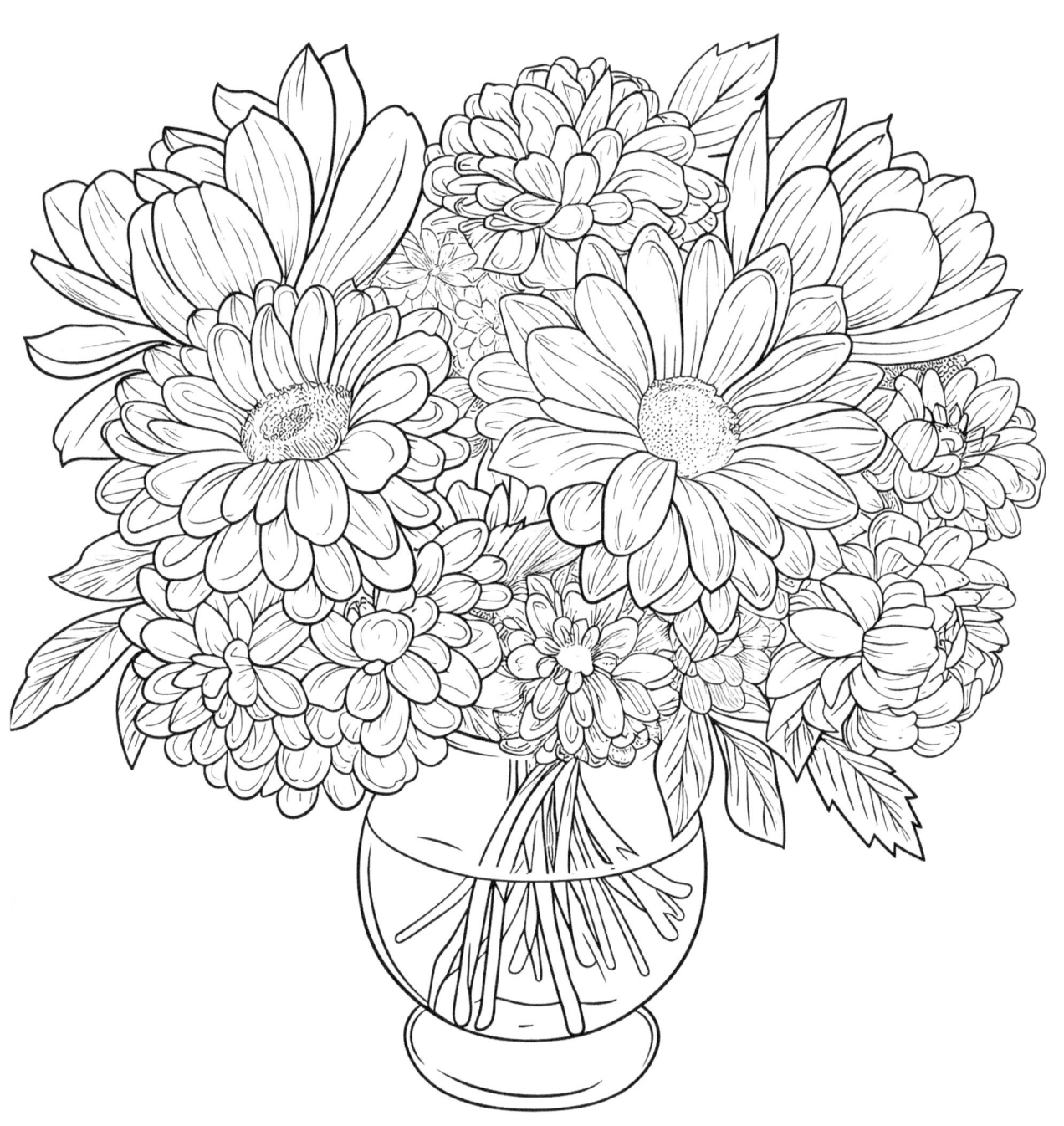

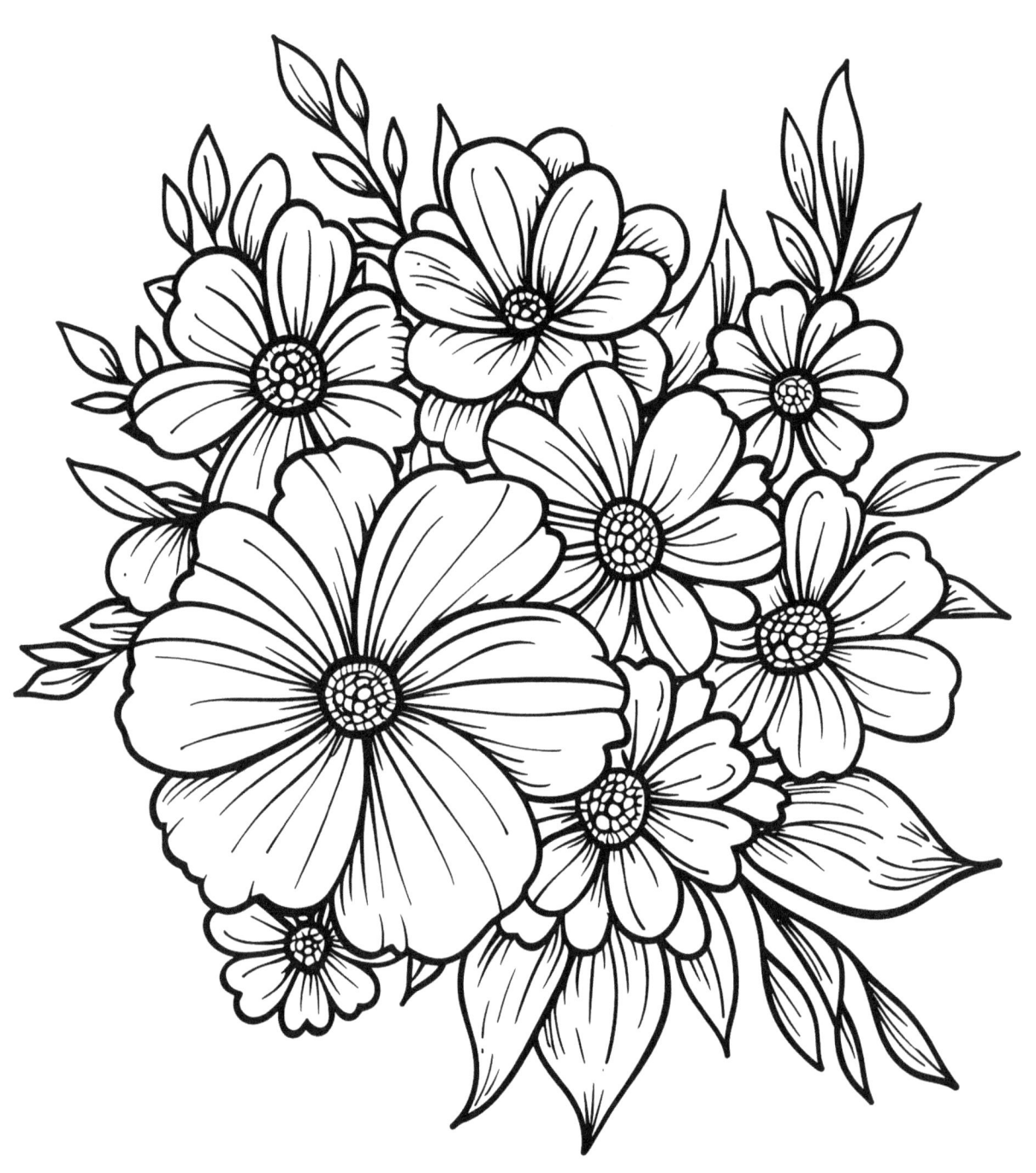

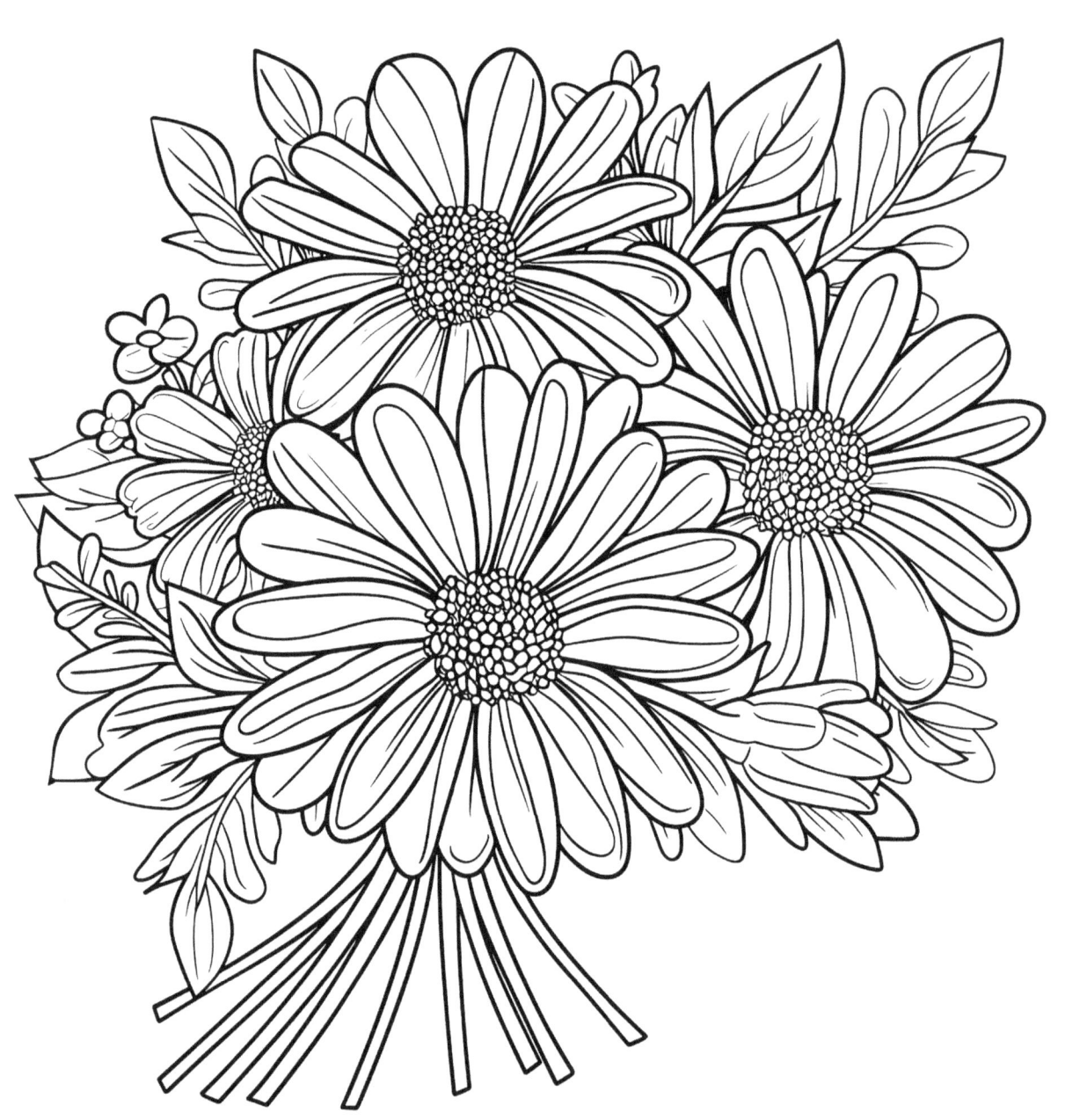

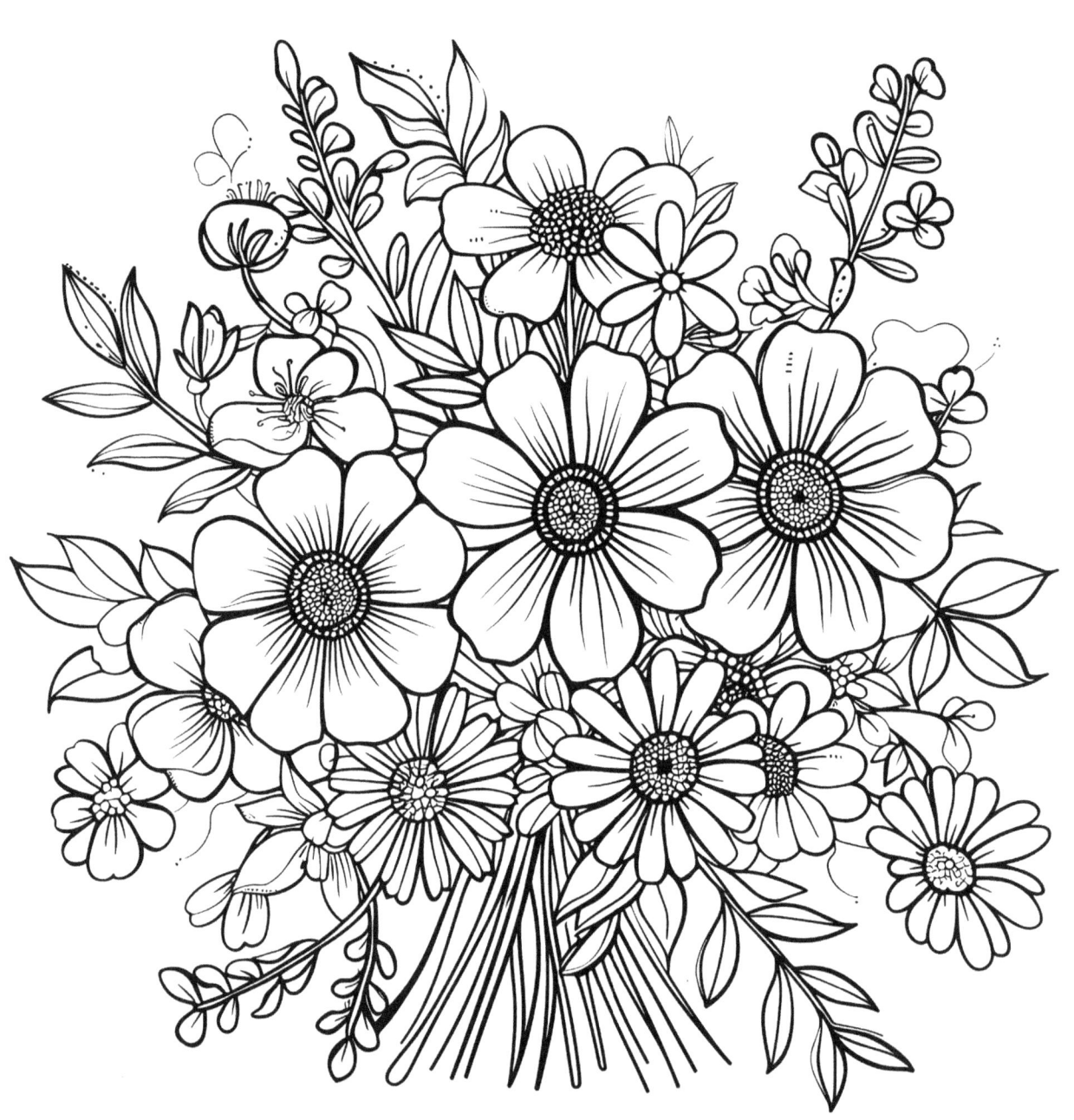

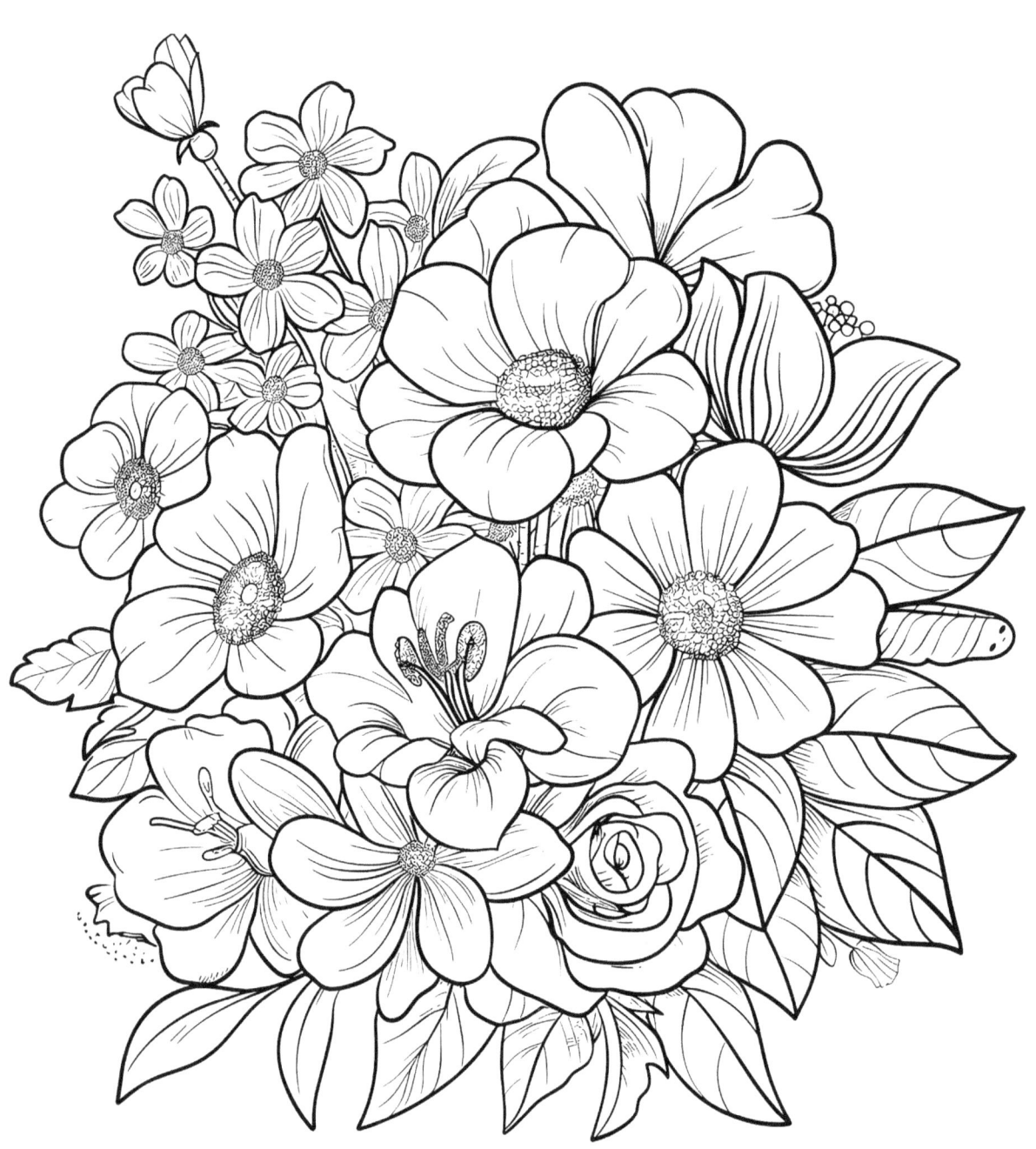

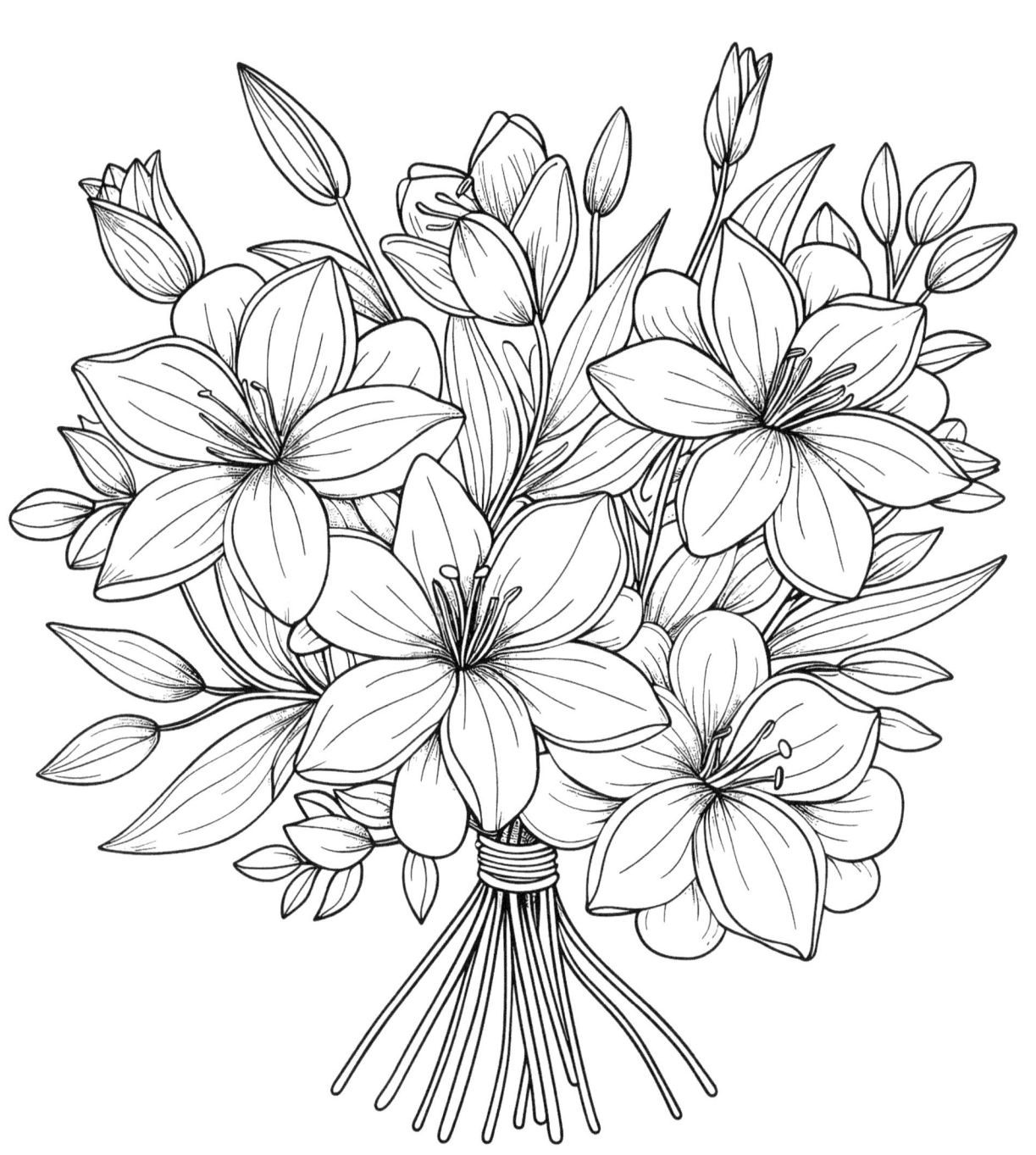

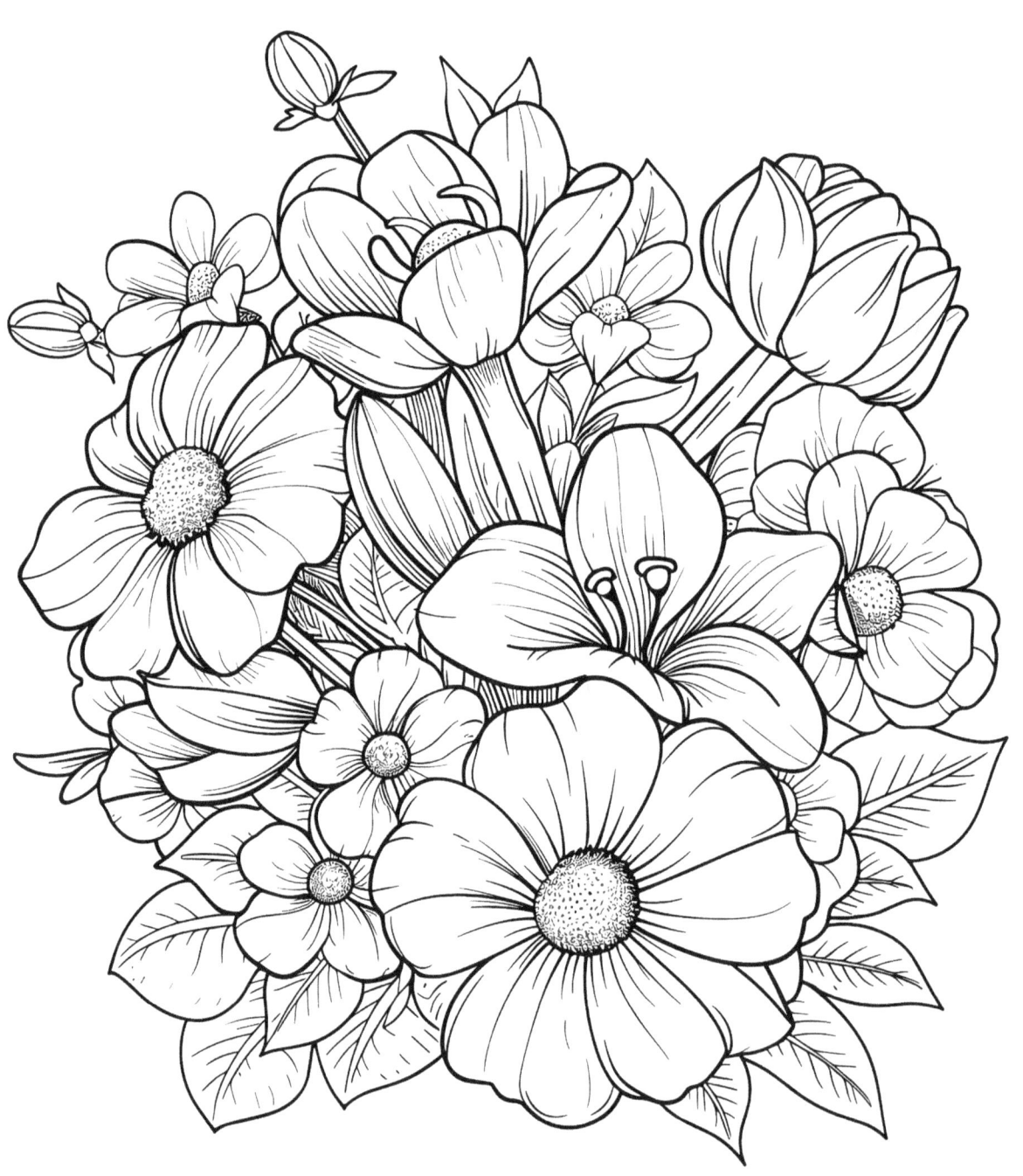

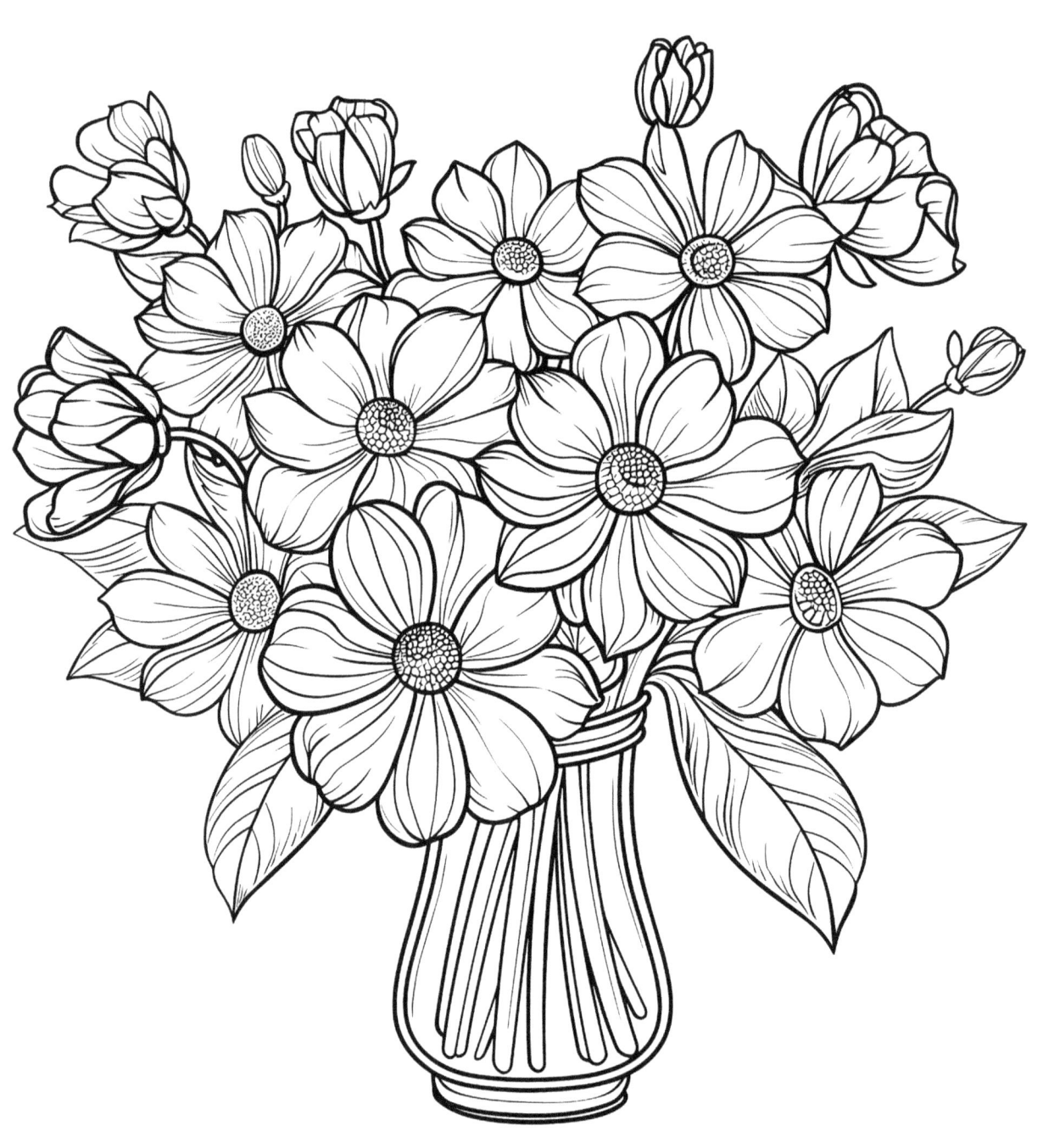

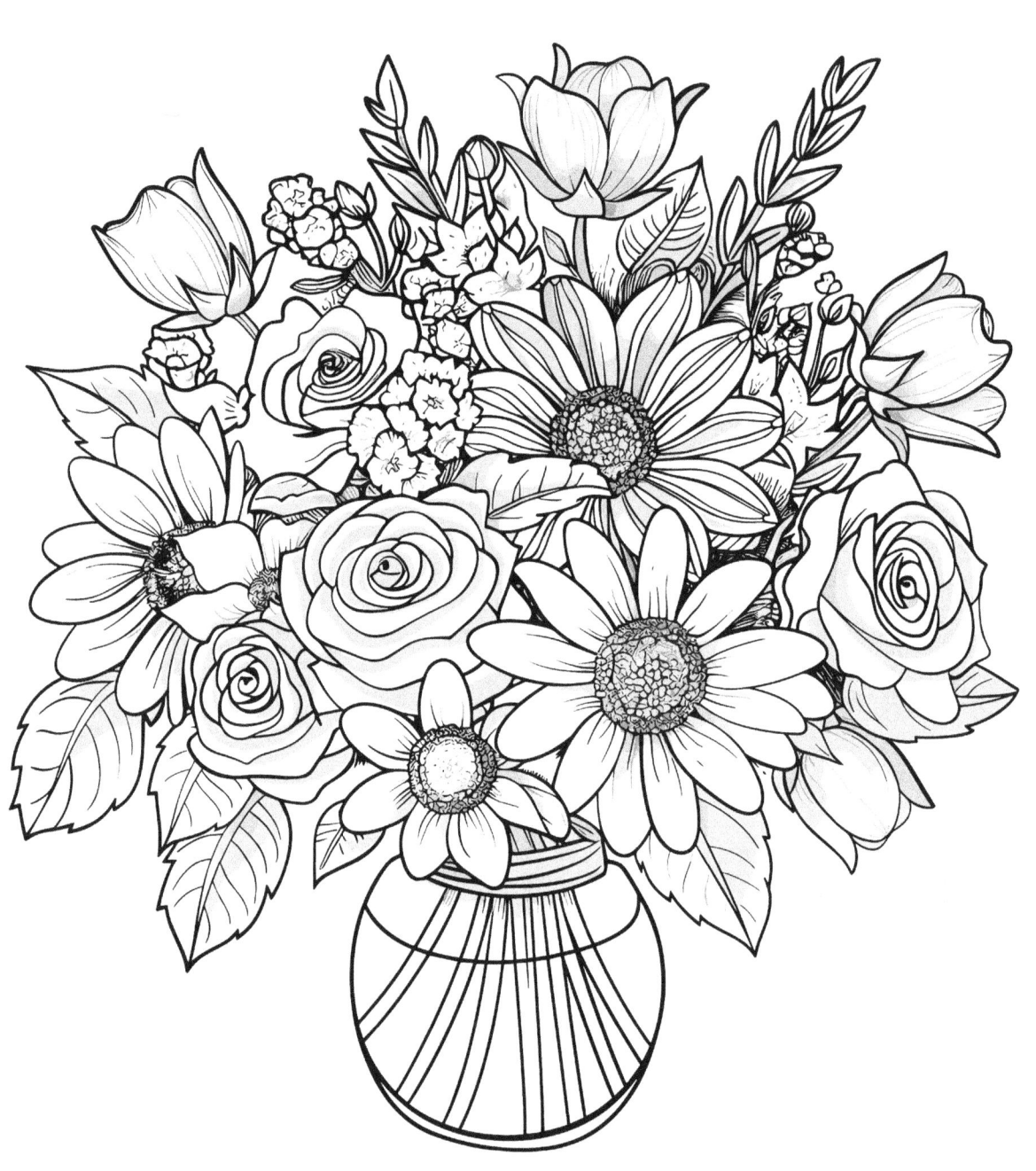

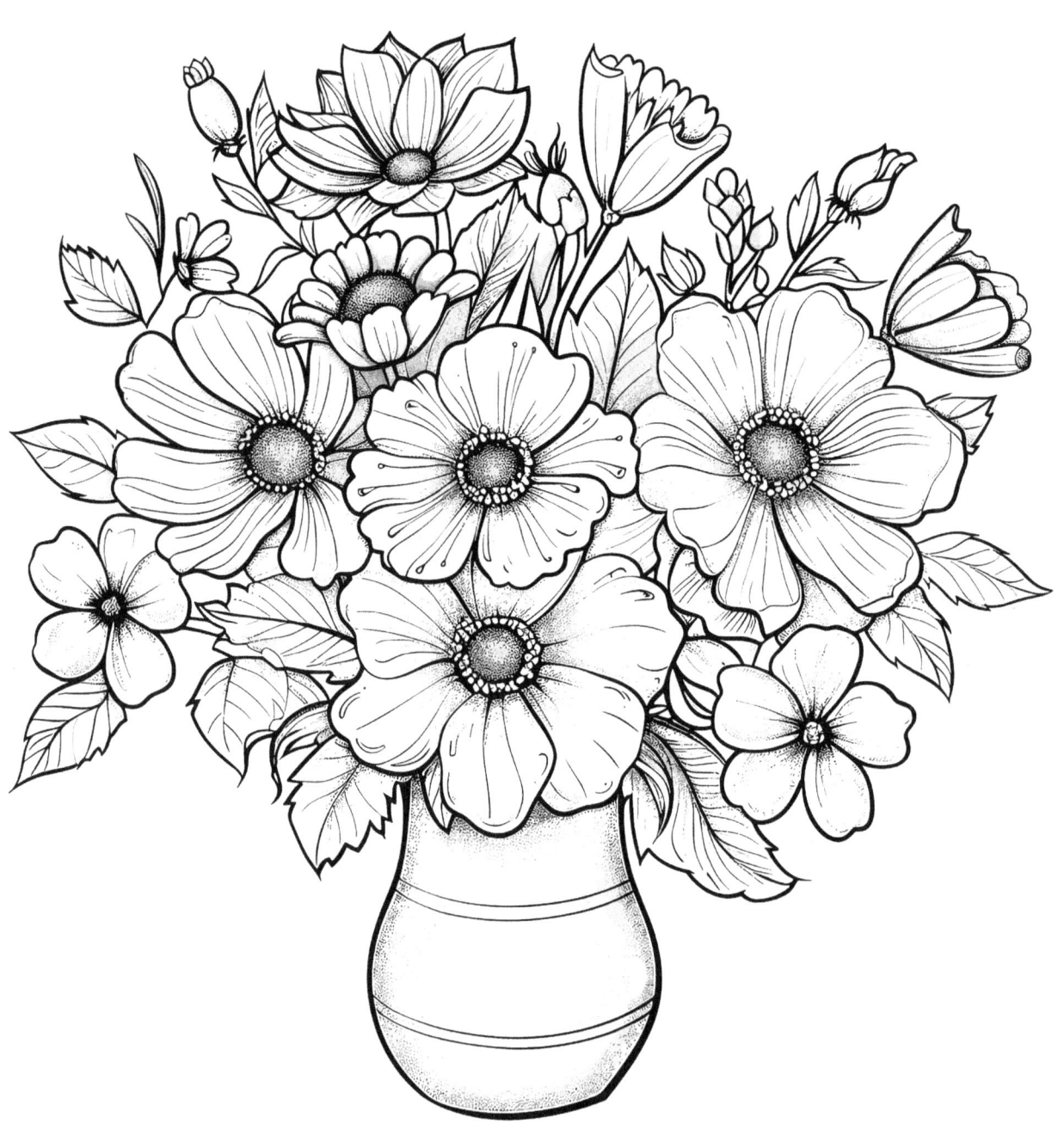

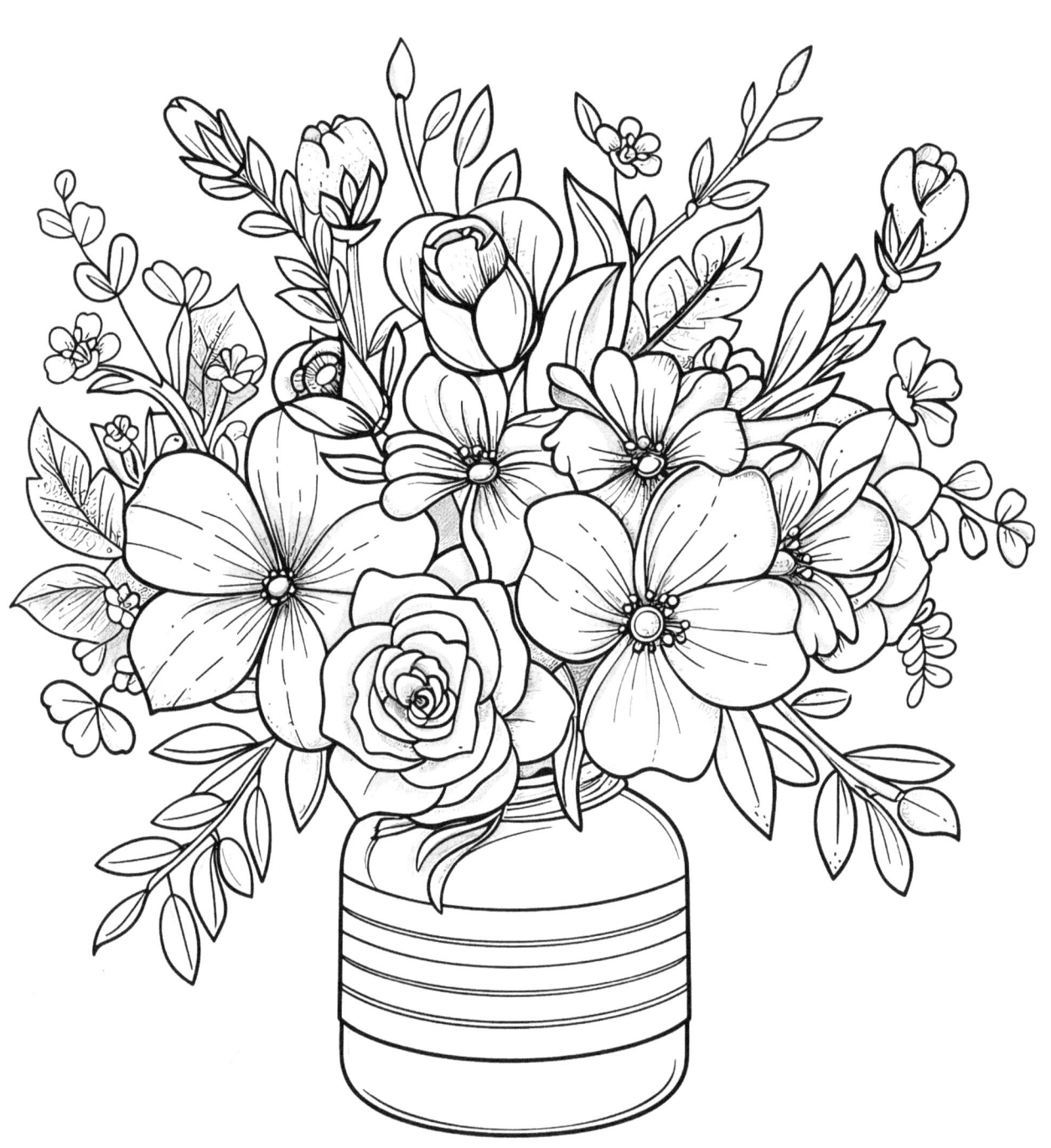

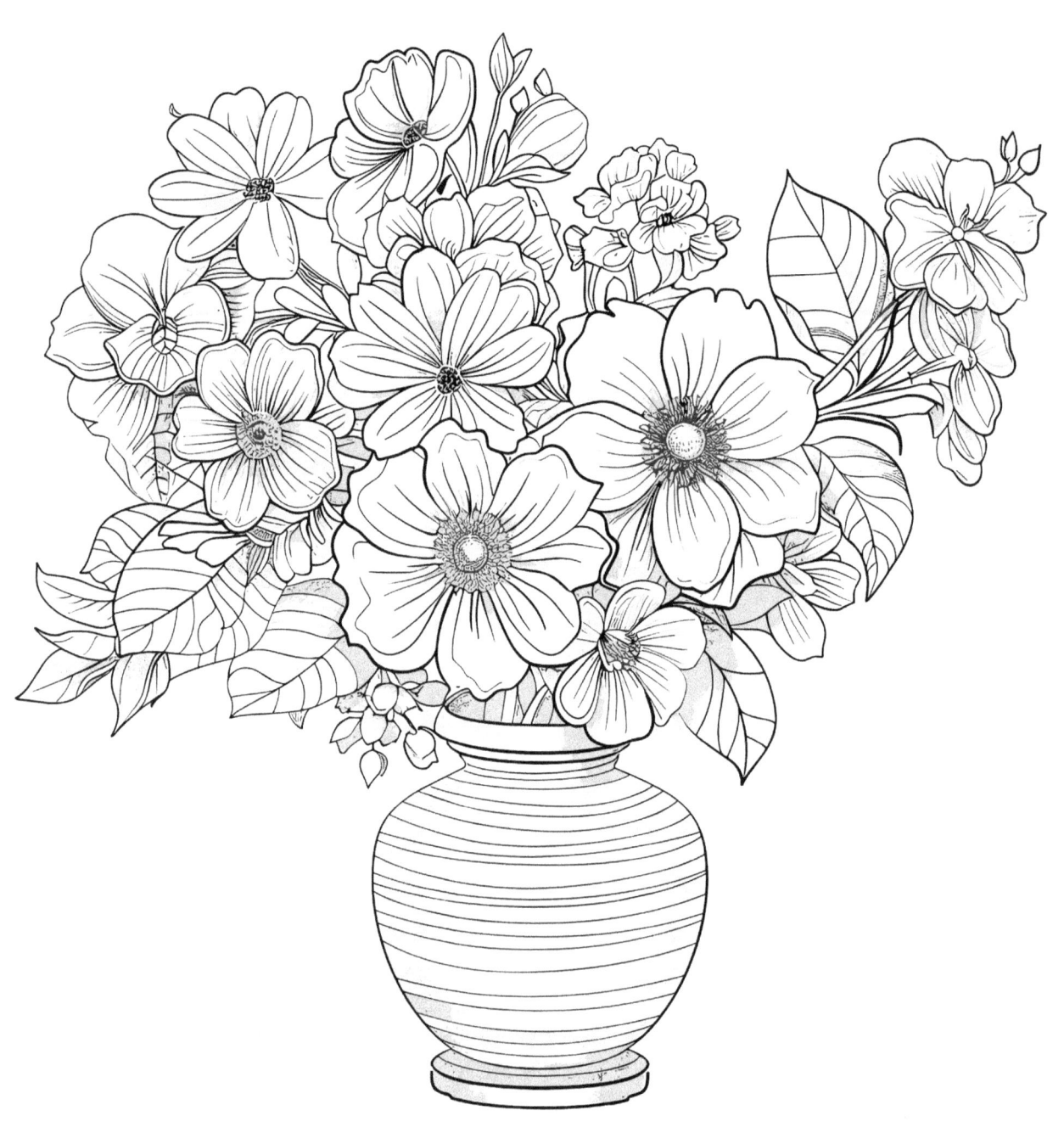

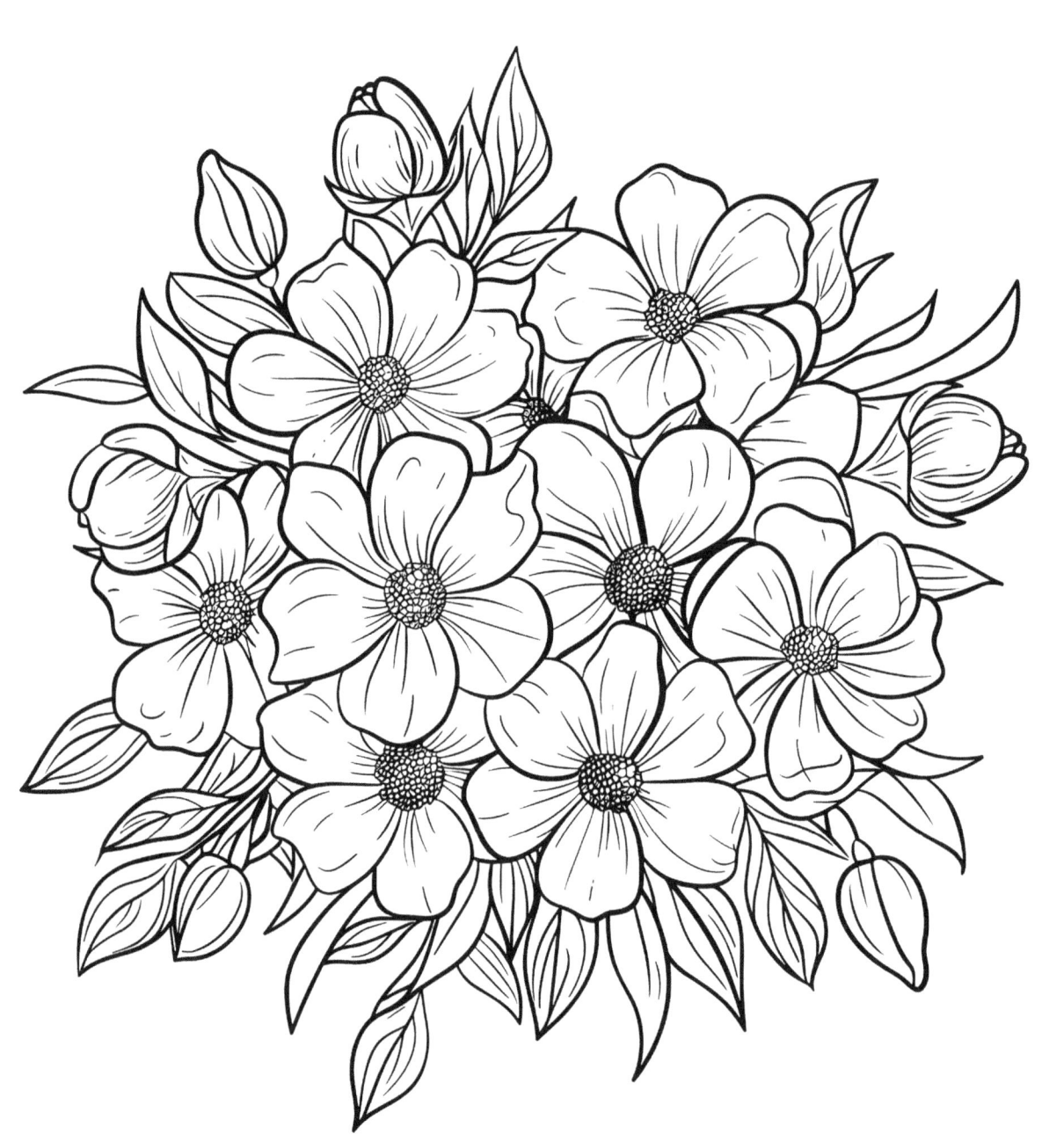

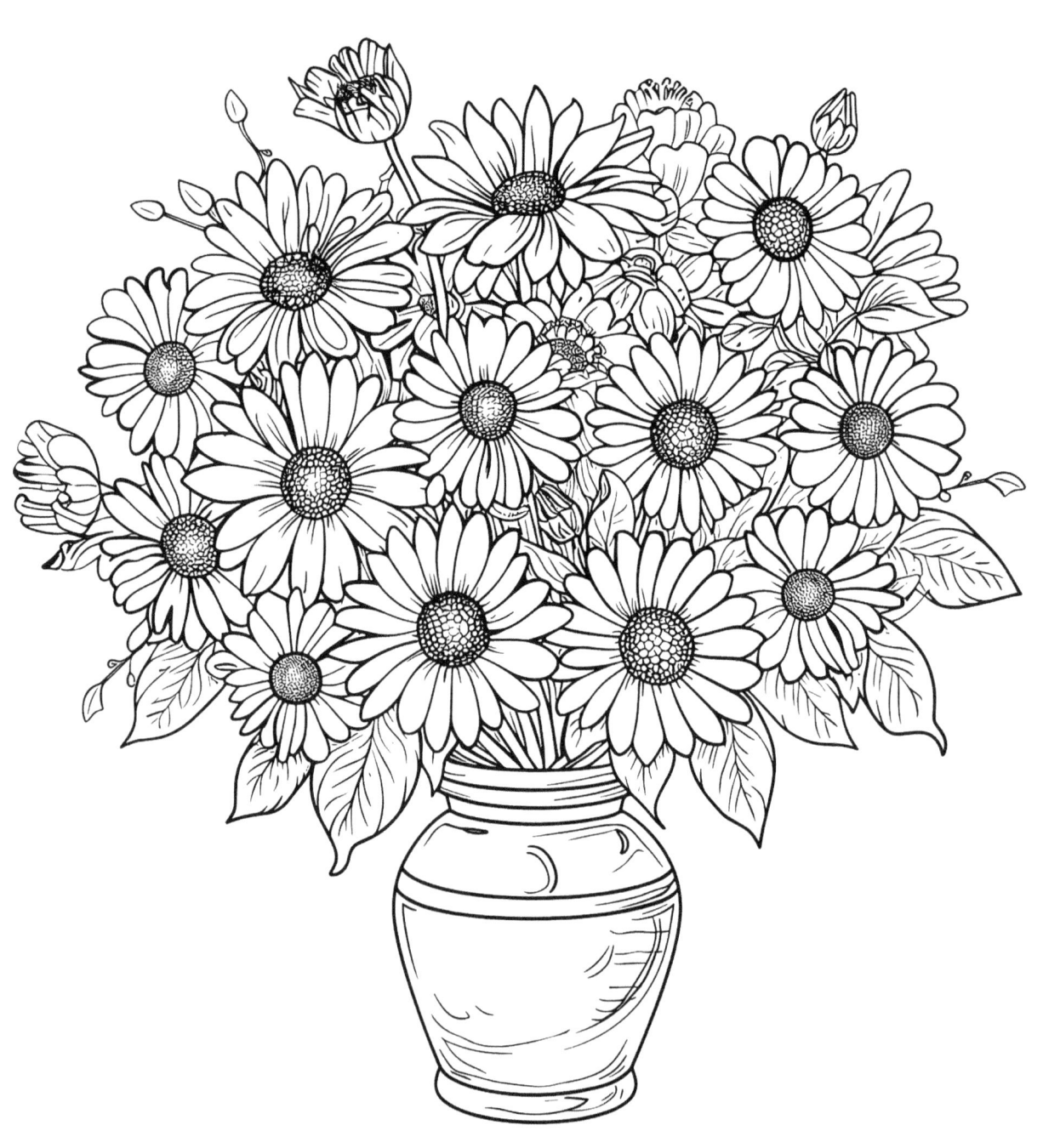

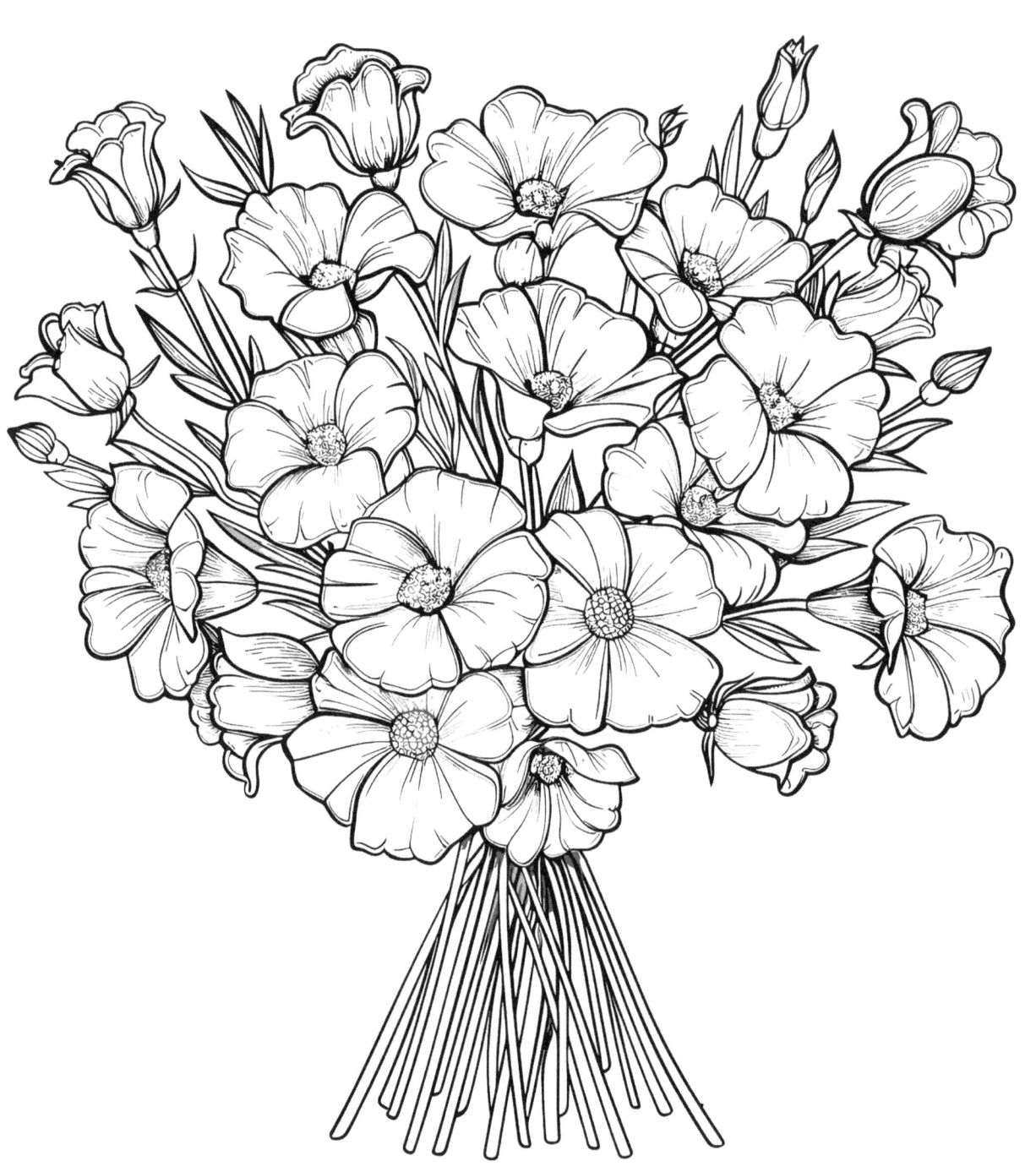

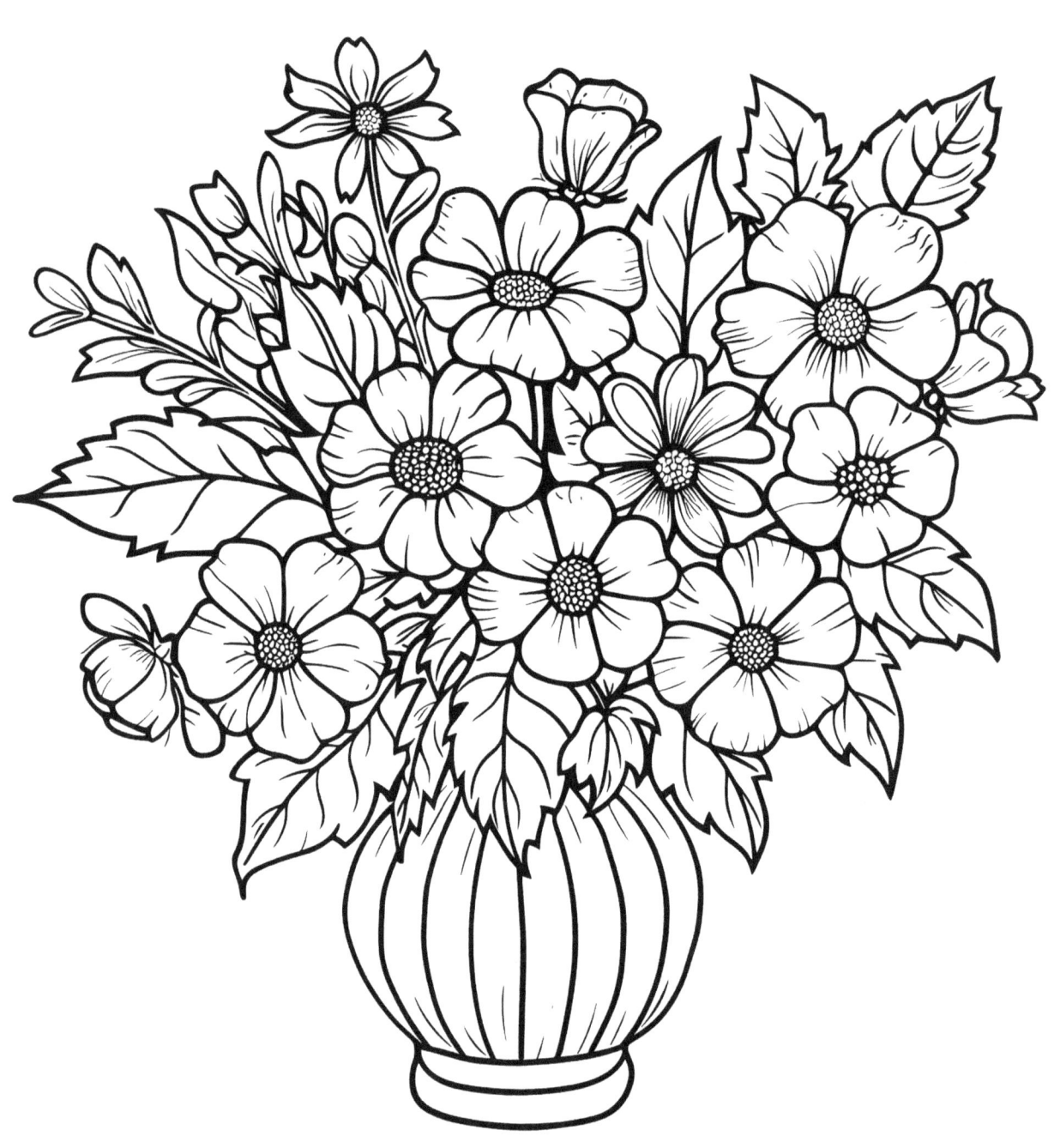

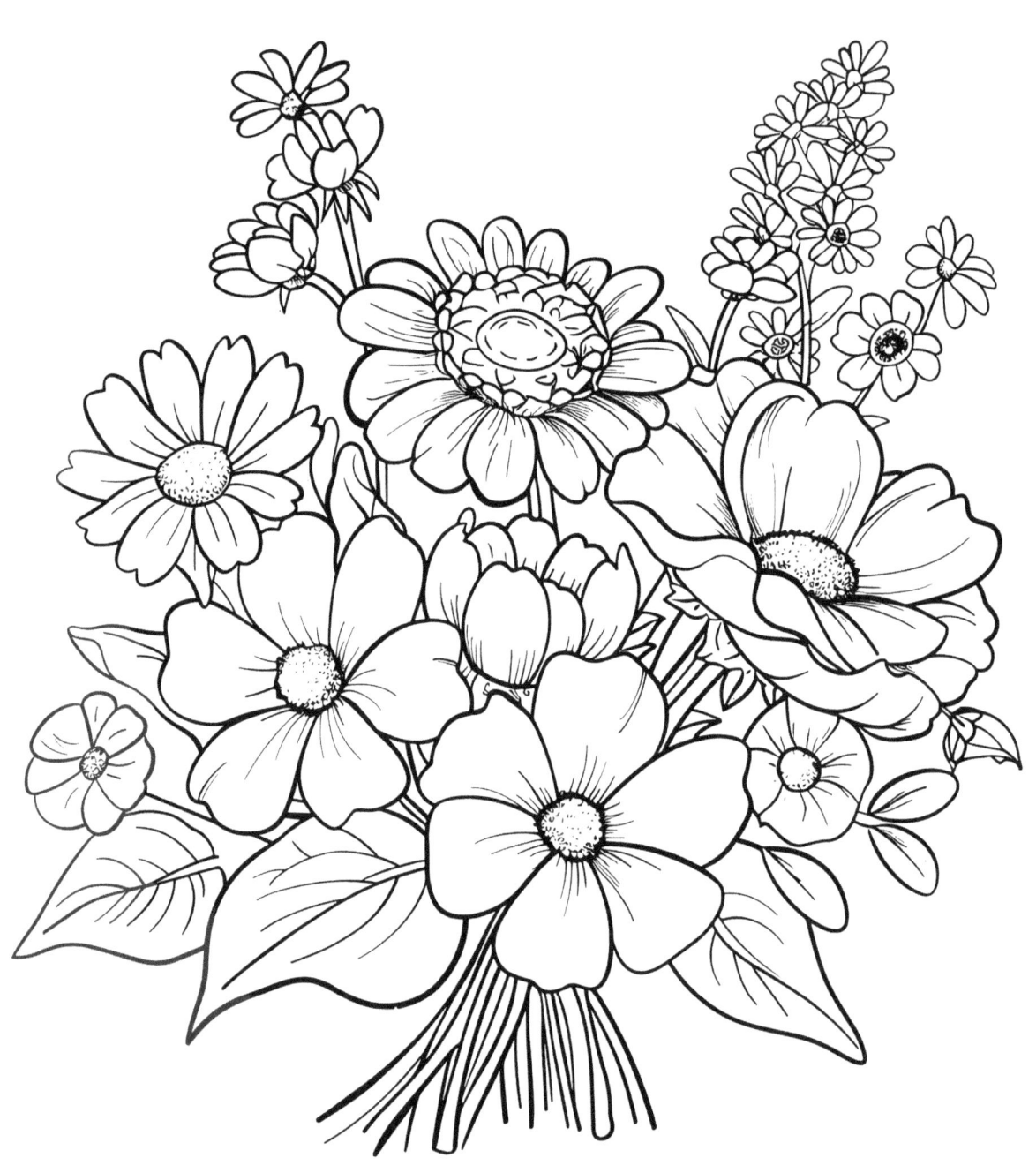

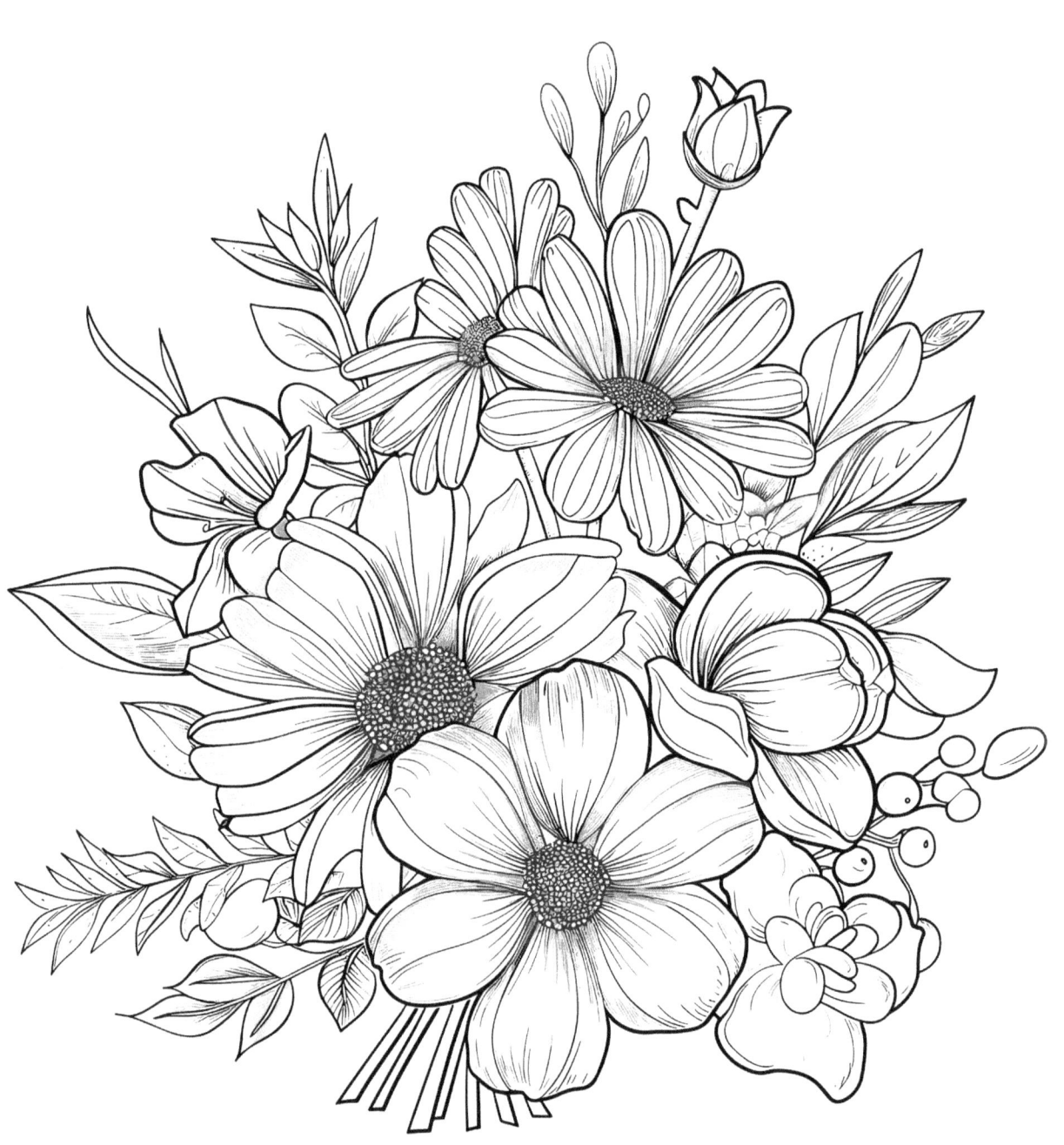

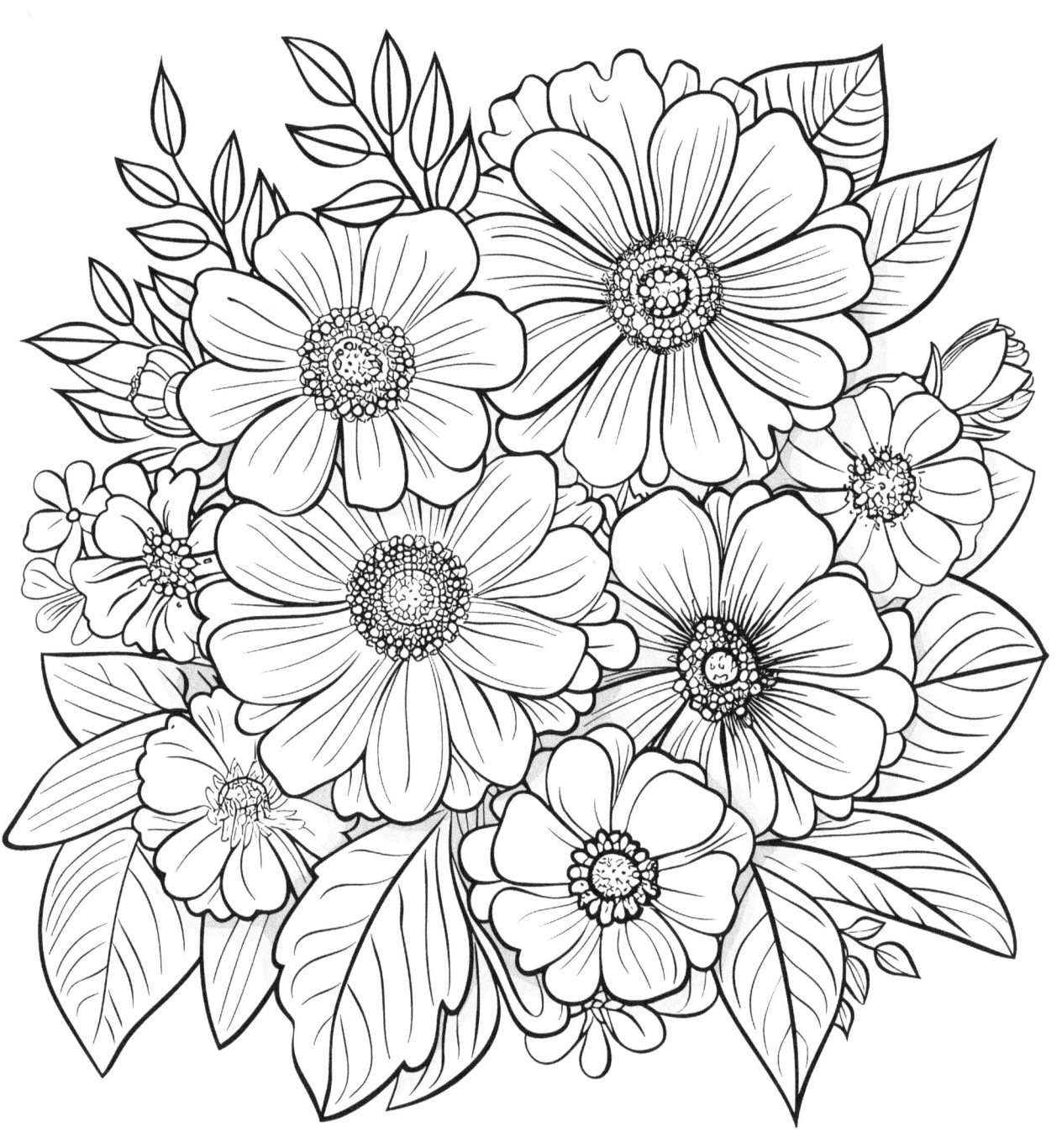

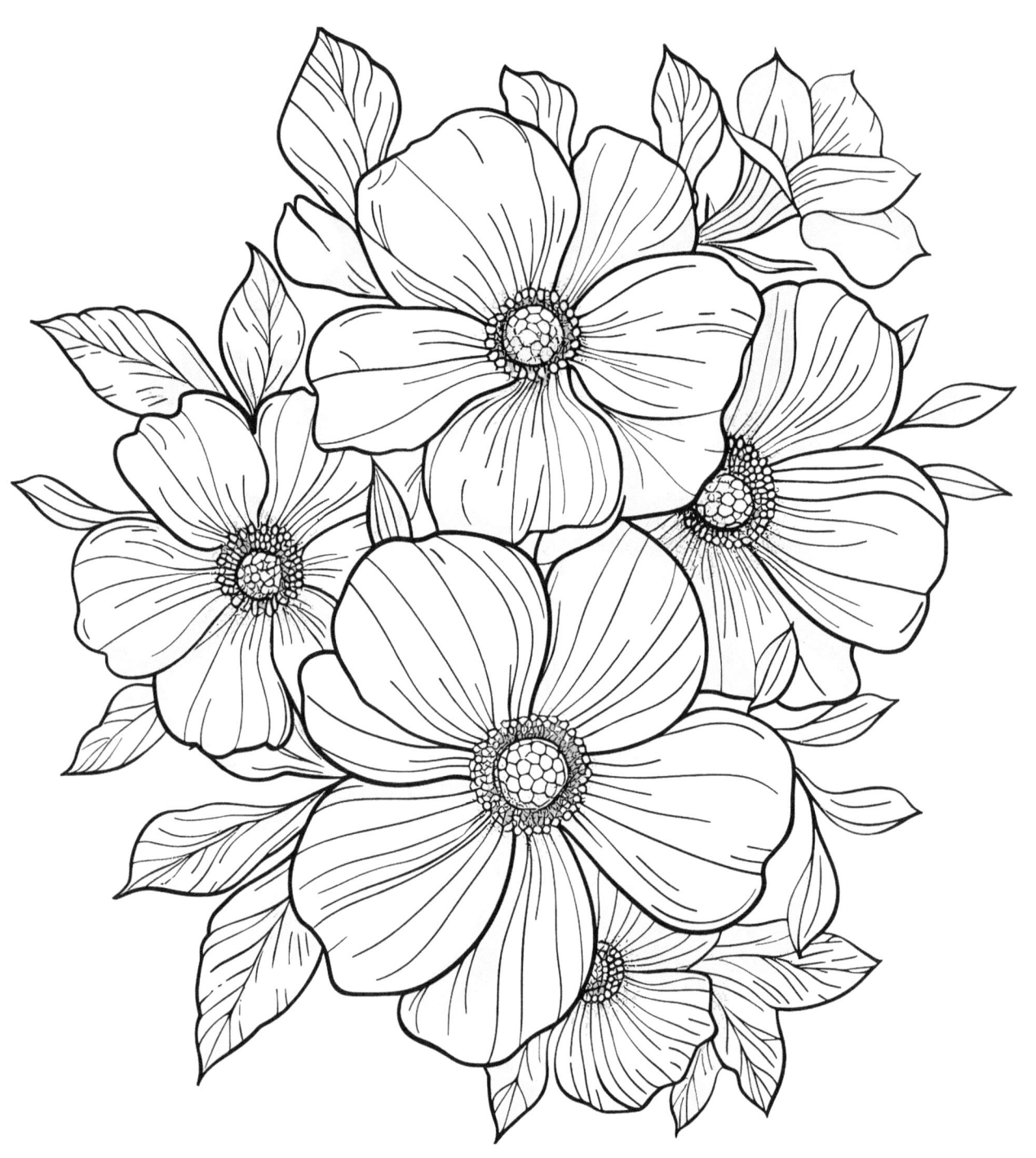

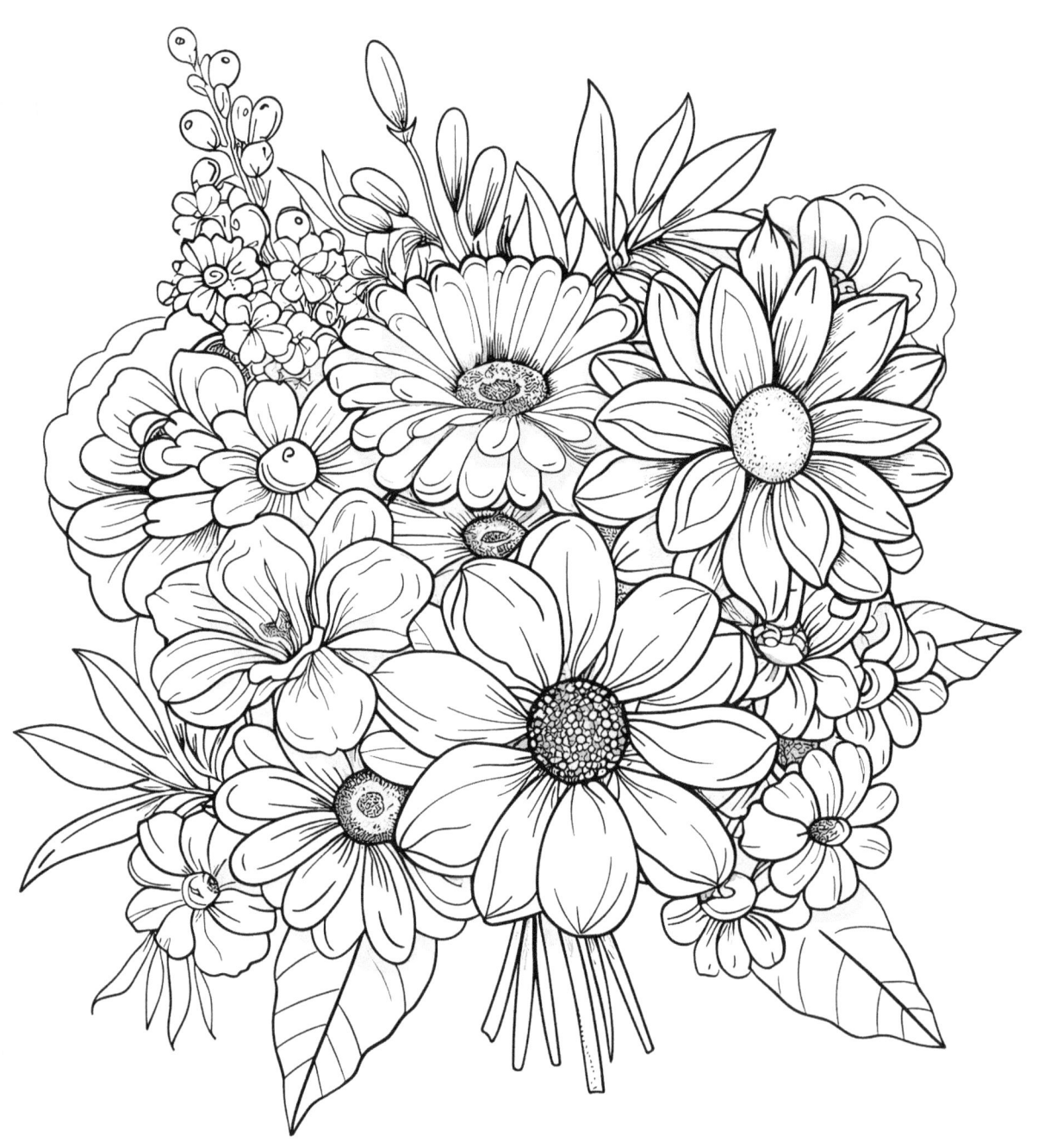

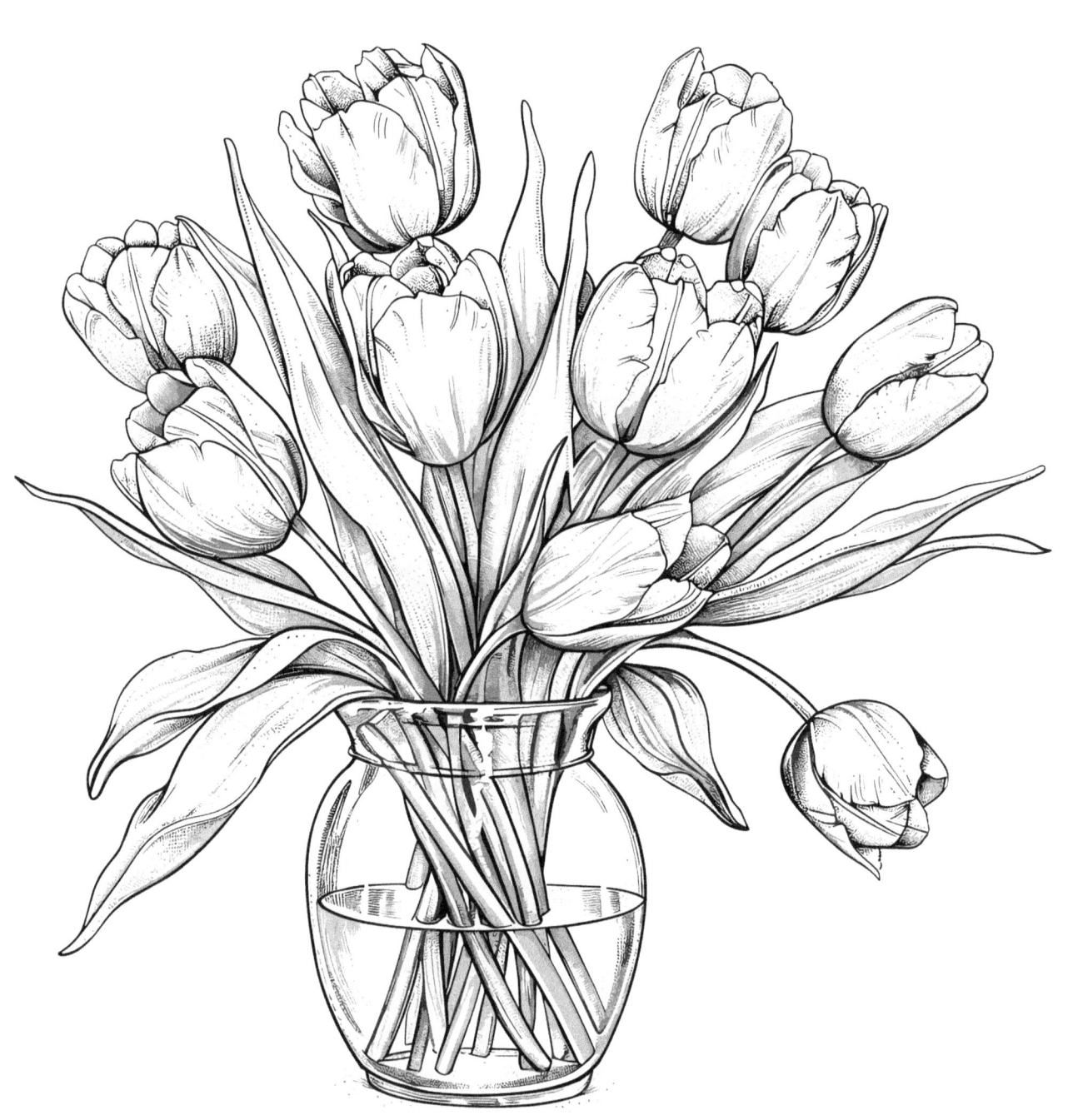

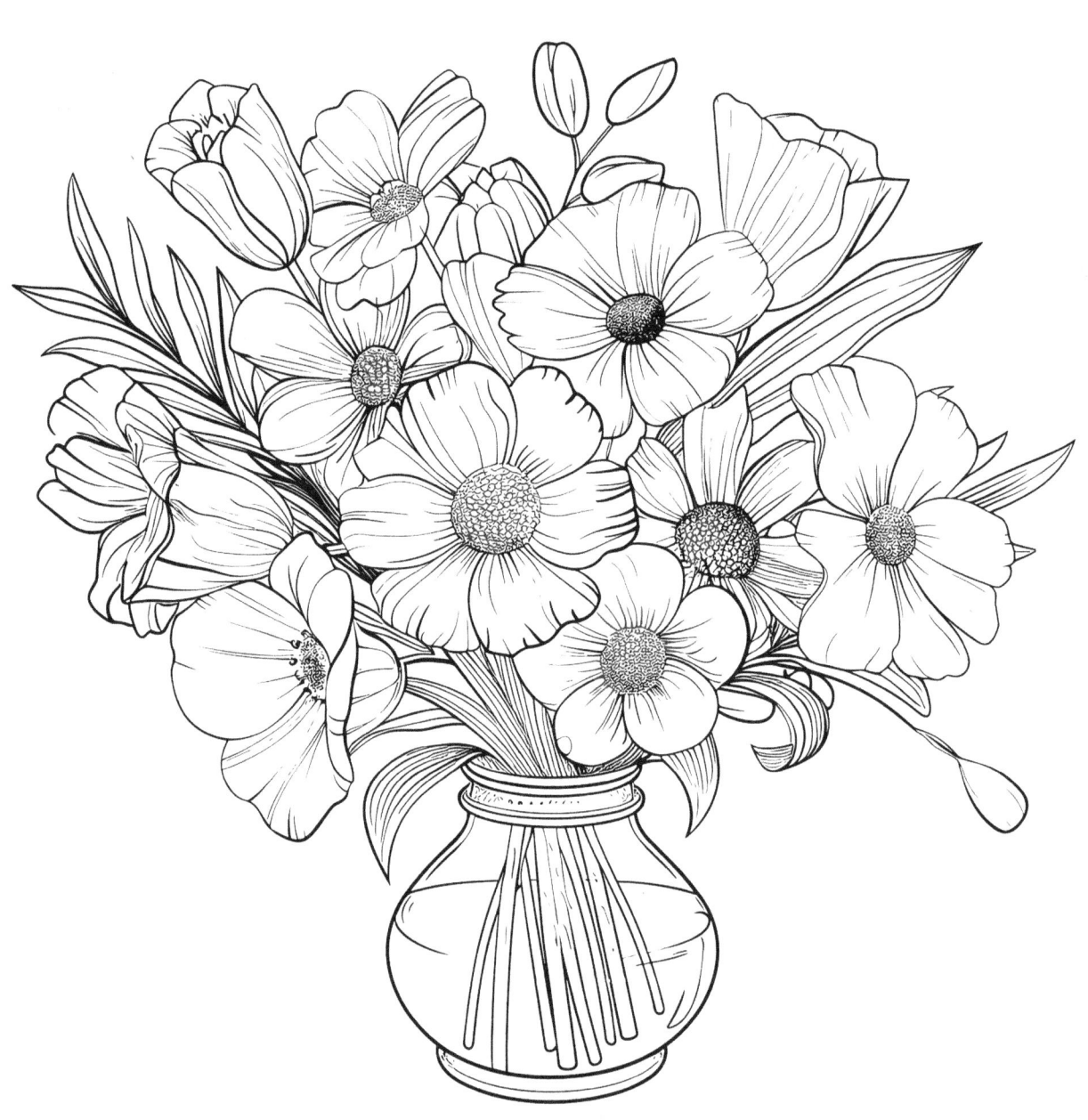

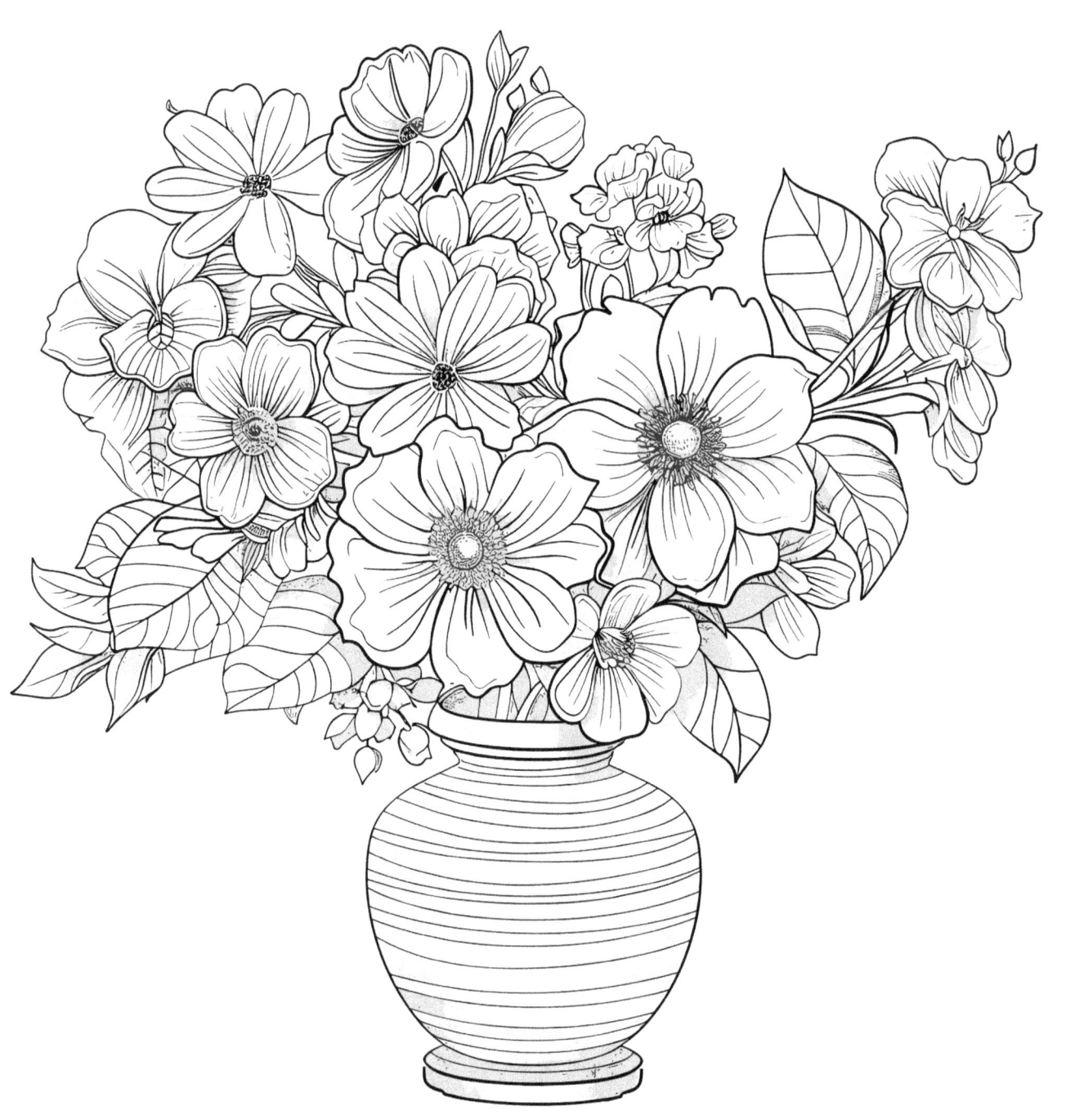

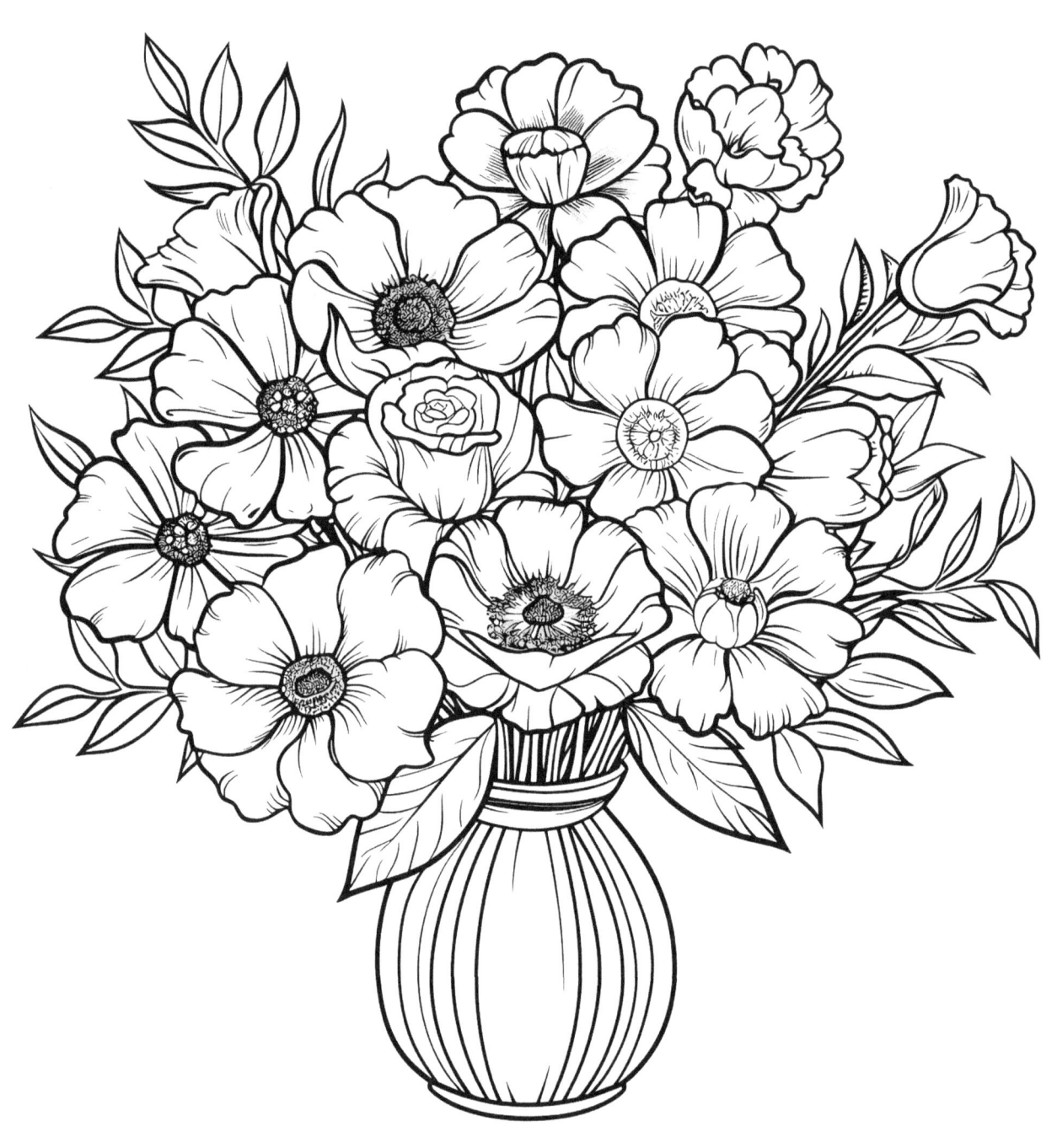

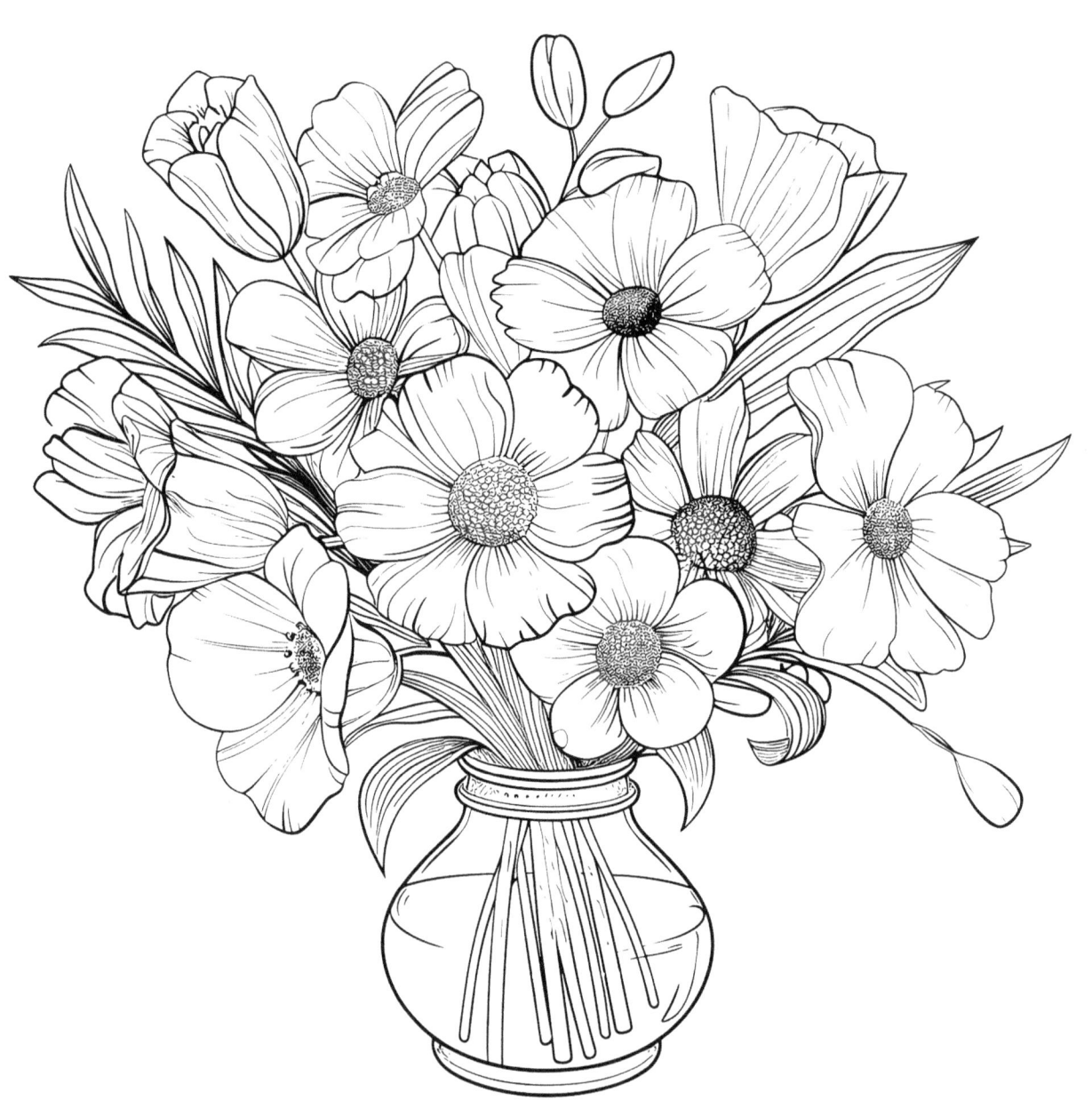